FROM THE HANDS OF THE HILLS

Contents

Publisher: J.S. Uberoi
Text: Margaret Campbell
Photographs: Chusak Voraphitak
Original research: Nakorn Pongnoi
Editor: Sherry Brydson
Design: Bert Gallardo
Production Co-ordination: M.Mohindar

Media Transasia Limited,
1903—1905, Tai Sang Commercial Building,
24—34 Hennessy Road, Hong Kong.

Printed in Hong Kong by: Toppan Printing Co. (HK) Ltd.

Media Transasia

ABOUT THE AUTHORS

MARGARET CAMPBELL first became interested in Hilltribe handicrafts when she worked in the Thai Hill-Crafts Foundation's retail shop in Bangkok as a volunteer. Sensing her interest, the Foundation encouraged her to start the research on the book, and eventually to write the text. She has an M.A. in English Literature from Dalhousie University in Halifax, Nova Scotia, Canada. Prior to her arrival in Thailand she taught English at Simon Fraser University in New Westminster, British Columbia.

NAKORN PONGNOI has been interested in producing a book on the Hilltribes since 1966, when he began to work in the hill areas of Thailand as a teacher, development officer and educational advisor. He has been responsible for making the necessary contacts with the tribespeople as well as for collecting the legends and folkways described in the book. After obtaining a B.A. in Education from Chulalongkorn University in Bangkok, he went to the United States on a Fulbright Scholarship, attending Stanford University and San Francisco State University, where he received an M.A. in Education.

CHUSAK VORAPHITAK has a B.A. from Chulalongkorn University in Bangkok, Thailand. During his second year at university he became seriously interested in photography, and in 1973 won H.R.H. Princess Maha Chakri Sirindhorn's Cup in a nationwide university photographic competition. In 1975 he took eight prizes in the prestigious Tourist Organization of Thailand photographic competition, including first, second and third prizes. He has spent one and a half years taking the photographs for this book.

THE THAI HILL-CRAFTS FOUNDATION

THE THAI HILL-CRAFTS Foundation is a private, non-profit, non-political organization formed under the patronage of H.R.H. the Princess Mother.

It seeks to promote and preserve each tribal craft as well as sponsoring projects in adult education.

The Foundation believes that the hill people have the right and ability to help determine their own futures. They play an integral role in the planning and programmes of the Foundation.

FOREWORD

THERE IS SO little written information available about the crafts of the hilltribes that almost all the details contained in the following pages have been gathered through interviews, either with hilltribe people or with outsiders who have lived and worked among the tribes for many years.

To the hilltribe people, I offer the book itself as a gift. I hope it will convey my thanks for their assistance by recording for the first time the beauty of their handiwork. Royalties from the book go to the Thai Hill-Crafts Foundation.

To the "outsiders" I would like to say a warm thank you. Very special mention must be made of two people. Khun Nakorn Pongnoi first suggested writing this book and in the two years it has taken to prepare he has been an unfailing source of encouragement and information, often making long trips into the hills to check and cross-check for me. He has spent many months guiding the photographer, Khun Chusak Voraphitak, to various villages and suggesting which crafts should be photographed. His assistance as interpreter has been invaluable to both Chusak and myself.

Mrs. Elaine Lewis of Chiang Mai has been my other source of help and enthusiasm. She put her extensive knowledge of the Lahu, Lisu and Akha crafts at my disposal, and spent many hours correcting the manuscript and cross-checking details.

Much of the credit for this book goes to these people.

Other people who have given generously their time and knowledge are too numerous to name, but to all of them — thank you. My particular thanks to Lois Calloway for sharing her experience of the Yao, Doris Dickerson for her help with details about Karen crafts, Ron Morse for his information about the Lisu, and Gordon Young for his stories about living and hunting with the Lahu. I would also like to toss a bouquet to Richard Strachan for focussing my attention on the need to capture the "atmosphere" of the hills, and to Wendy Strachan for untangling my syntax and pointing out obscurities.

And deepest thanks to my husband Roger without whose interest, criticisms and unfailing support the task could never have been completed.

Margaret Campbell
Bangkok, June 1976

MOST OF THE research on this book was done while I was working with the Thai Hill-Crafts Foundation. During this period, the members of the Board showed great insight into the importance of preserving the hilltribe culture, and understood that the procedure takes time and care. I am grateful to the Board members, M.R. Disnada Diskul, Mr. Apilas Osatananda, Mr. Chiochan Kriengsiri, Mrs. Poonsri Thongkaimok, Mrs. Pakapan Meecharoen and Mr. Glen Dunkley for their encouragement and support throughout this project.

I would also like to thank the Border Patrol Police Area V, the Siam Society, M.R. Patrasuk Jocusri, Mr. Sanit Woongprasert, Mr. Somphop Larchrojana, Mrs. Duangjit Thaweesri, Mr. Choomporn Wongsawat, Mr. Somchai Pakdiphuwadon, Mrs. Kulthida Boon-it, Ms. Joslyn Grassby and Mr. Jeremy Hepworth for their generous help.

And I want to express my gratitude to Sherry Brydson, who has been more than just an editor.

Nakorn Pongnoi
Bangkok, April 1977

WRITING A book of this scope is no easy task. It was put together over a period of nearly three years by a team of four culturally (and often geographically) diverse people who drove, flew and walked over most of northern Thailand to collect the data presented here.

The book started as a relatively modest effort when Nakorn Pongnoi of the Thai Hill-Crafts Foundation asked Margaret Campbell, the wife of a Canadian University Students Overseas (CUSO) field officer stationed in Bangkok, to write the text to accompany a pictorial book about the handicrafts which are the main concern of the Foundation. For the next 18 months, Margaret visited museums, universities and libraries, conducted interviews with anthropologists and missionaries and visited hilltribe villages to assemble the material for the book.

Meanwhile, photographer Chusak Voraphitak undertook the task of photographing the finest hillcrafts in the villages where they are made. For more than two years, Chusak donated his services, often walking for two days to remote villages to photograph special costumes or rare ceremonies. His enthusiasm never flagged.

Throughout the three-year period, Nakorn acted as co-ordinator, guide, translator and field researcher. By the time Margaret had completed her manuscript and returned to Canada, he had assembled a briefcase full of new information: legends, poems, customs, ceremonies. There followed a six-month stretch in which Nakorn and I worked together to piece this new data into the book.

At this point we might well have given up in despair had it not been for the encouragement and sustained enthusiasm of publisher J.S. Uberoi, who insisted we turn this into a real "art" book and whose Bangkok office we turned into a battleground week after week as we sorted the best pictures from a collection of more than 10,000. And when we had fitted the bits and pieces together for the last time, Peangchai Abhiradee took time from other pressing duties to re-type our crazy-quilt manuscript.

I am proud to have been a part of such a magnificent effort.

Sherry Brydson
Bangkok, April 1977

The earth was created a little too large and the heaven was a little too small. Strings were attached to the four corners of the earth and were drawn, forming hills and valleys. Rocks and stones were put in. Seeds of trees and plants were sown to make the birds happy and sing for joy. The hills in their beauty shone . . . .

The Creation of the Earth (Lahu narrative)

In the mountains of

Northern Thailand there is a village.

IT IS THE home of people who have wandered through the mountains of southern China, Burma, Laos and Thailand for hundreds of years. Their language and dress is that of their tribe, their homeland is the mountains, their allegiance is to their headman, and their greatest fear is of the evil spirits that lurk in the jungle, the waters and even in the rice fields.

The village sits close to the crest of a hill. The houses are low and modest, merging with the contours of the land, the roofs of cogon grass* thatch and bamboo walls hardly distinguishable from the packed earth trails and cleared ground that surround them. It might belong to any of the tribes who live in these parts, for although each group is now quite unrelated to any of the others, they share a simple lifestyle. It seems a peaceful place.

There are women working in the fields, singing softly as they weed. From girls to grandmothers, they are all here, for this is women's work. From time to time, snatches of their song drift back to the village. Most of the young matrons have babies tied on their backs, snoozing quietly. Only one is objecting, wailing loudly and refusing to be lulled to the crooning of his mother and sisters. He is hungry and his mother will have to open her blouse for him, or the whole group will have no peace.

Grandfather, from his vantage point in the shade, puts aside his pipe and glares across the valley of the sound of the distant wail. Each succeeding generation has a louder voice, it seems! He resumes his puffing and turns his attention back to the top spinning contest that is in progress. The tops are made of hardwood, only roughly carved, but challenges and counter-challenges occupy the boys for hours every day. Grandfather finds it all most stimulating.

Which is more than can be said for his other encounters with these youngsters! Some of them have been to school and others have made journeys to towns bigger than any he has ever seen, and once outside the family circle they tend to ignore the old ways and imitate the people from the lowlands. After all, it's not as though the school can teach them anything of their own history, or even their own language — only the elders can do that — yet they seem to think that schoolbooks with their incomprehensive pictures are more important.

All their talk these days is of towns with houses taller than the tallest trees in the jungle, of how hard it is to learn the new language — and of new kinds of clothes. They want to discard the comfortable, practical clothes of their ancestors and deck themselves out in T-shirts and leather shoes. Fortunately most of them have little money and mothers with lots of common sense, so they are still wearing decent clothes, home-spun and handmade and decorated with love by the women. But that doesn't stop them dreaming. Their great hero is the dare-devil from the next village who made his way right to the city and persuaded the people at the radio station that he had a wonderful new song for them. The radio people recorded it enthusiastically and broadcast to

every transistor in the hills his "singing letter", sending greetings to all his friends, news of his adventures in the big town, and descriptions of all the amazing things he'd seen. Since then, every young male in the tribe has been restless.

Grandfather pulls deeply on his pipe. He has tried to economise by mixing tobacco with the residue scraped from his opium pipe, and it is tangy but not really satisfying. Maybe later he'll indulge in a proper smoke of opium. There are so many aches and pains these days and opium is the best medicine, better than herbs from the jungle or pills from the town. If outsiders ever persuade the headman to stop growing opium — and every day the pressure increases — there will be no solace for the suffering. It is comforting to know that when all else fails, there is always opium. He remembers the long cruel illness that killed his wife. Opium was her salvation, as it is now his. Yet even here, so far from a town, someone is always telling them to give up their opium growing and try new crops. New seeds appear and strangers give mystifying talks on how to plant them. But even if they grow — and many of them don't because no one has the time to take care of them — none is as practical and portable as opium. Why should a farmer grow a hundredweight of some crop and walk five days to the nearest market when he can earn the same money selling one pocketful of opium to the eager traders who come regularly to the village!

Yet the younger men seem to be talking seriously of alternatives. And his son is always talking about a shortage of land, too, and laws forbidding the cutting of more forest. Ridiculous! Just look around — still plenty of tree-covered hills, and who is to know if a man cuts down a tree anyway. There is always more land and always more trees, and if you do not cut and burn the trees and the undergrowth, the crops will never grow well. Once an outsider came with some white powder called "fertiliser" and told them to put that on the land instead, but everyone knew by the feel that it was not ash and would do no good, so they left the sack under the house and burned the fields as usual. And everything grew well. It always does, unless the spirits are offended and then no amount of white powder can help to make the crops strong.

The thought of angry spirits makes the old man glance warily at the split bamboo aqueducts running through the village. He still does not feel happy about bringing the water spirits so close to the house, but although he fought and argued tenaciously younger heads prevailed on that issue and most of the villagers hailed it as a modern innovation and revelled in the touch of luxury that brought clear water right to the door. The women were certainly glad not to have to carry the heavy bamboo water containers home every day. Yet Grandfather cannot help shaking his head and worrying about the unnecessary risk they are running. Water spirits are powerful and often malevolent, and inviting them right into the village is so dangerous.

Ah well, it is almost time to move again so maybe in the

*Imperative Cyclindrica Koenigii

new village the argument can be fought again and maybe this time he will win. That will be something to look forward to. The village has been settled here twelve — no, it must be fourteen — years now, so it is nearly time to go. And the trek has always been an exciting time too, with everyone from toddler to grandfather gathering their few belongings and setting off together, crossing streams and mountain passes, to the new site that the headman and the elders have chosen. Then the forest is cleared, houses built, crops planted — and it is back to smoking pipes. Yes, one more move before I die, he thinks contentedly; it is a satisfying ritual and I will enjoy doing it once more. Though there will be a special sadness in going too, for the grave of my wife will be left behind. . .

He begins to nod gently over his pipe. From a nearby house his daughter-in-law watches him thoughtfully. Her arms move constantly, stirring her homespun cloth into the dark blue dye she has made from the leaves and twigs of her indigo plant. In one corner of the house, her loom lies forsaken, its usefulness over for the moment. Piled in another corner are all the pieces of cloth it has produced, enough to make clothes for the whole family. They must be dyed to a deep rich colour — with a deep rich smell to match — and then sewn and decorated in time for the New Year celebrations. Everyone must have a new outfit for that occasion, but there are many weeks of work to be done before then. The daughters of the house have stayed home from the fields today to help with the dyeing and they are impatient to finish. The thought of a new outfit is an exciting one, for so much time and energy is put into making it that it must be saved for a special occasion. The new cloth brings promise of new beauty and already they are discussing how to decorate it. Tradition will dictate the basic style, of course, but there is always room for slight variations in colour or arrangement of design which enables them to show off their growing skills as craftswomen. Their mother listens to their happy plans with a small smile. She will be responsible for making clothes for all the men of the family as well as herself, and

When all else fails, there is always the pipe and the forgetfulness it brings.

Life in the village, thatched huts clinging to the hillsides and women at their chores.

Opium country. Magnificent, breathtaking and virtually isolated until twenty years ago.

Children wend their way home in the moonlight.
Typical village huts craddled by the hills.

17

Faces. A vignette of tribespeople in their traditional finery.

Hilltribe "Madonna and Child" relax by a pile of village firewood. An apprehensive child clutchces a spray of orchid blossoms. Village women go about their tasks.

22

Sunset over the hills auguring the end of an ancient way of life. Alternately pressured and prodded to abandon poppy cultivation in favour of other cash crops, the tradition-bound villagers are slow to adopt.

View of the hills blanketed by mist and wrapped in tranquility.

these frivolous daughters will have to help or the work will never get done in time. But she does not remind them of this. Young girls always manage to find time for the most elaborate adornments, no matter how many extra chores they are given, she reminisces to herself.

She glances back at the old man. He is almost 90 now, his long pigtail streaked with white to match his beard, his face weather-worn and deeply seamed, like a field parched by the sun. He will want new clothes too, even though he doesn't work now and hardly wears things out. Still he will take part in the celebrations as he has always done, and new clothes are a necessary part of the New Year ritual. And when the old ceremonies are performed and traditional costumes worn he will beam with pleasure again, reassured that the tribe is not losing its old ways after all. She hasn't dared tell him that she has sold some of her homespun cloth and some of her needlework to earn some money. He has complained often enough about others in the tribe squandering their heritage by selling their belongings, and she is afraid he will react the same way to her. But they have to eat all the food crops they grow and have none left over to sell, and now that virgin land is so scarce and cultivated land so exhausted, opium is becoming an unreliable source of cash. Selling crafts seems to offer a good way out, at least temporarily. The young men want transistor radios and guns, the girls want silver for jewelry and for their dowries. She stirs the pot rhythmically, wondering if she can manage to make a few extra things to sell from this batch of cloth.

A small man dressed all in black comes to the door. He is the village silversmith and he has come to borrow some live coals from the fire. Somehow his fire has gone out and already he is worrying about this bad omen. But he is easily persuaded to bring out his latest piece for the daughters to admire. It is a large silver neck ring, etched with delicate designs. He has made it for his own daughter so it is especially beautiful. For many years he has collected Indian rupees from the Yunnanese Chinese traders who wander through the hills and now he has melted them down to make her dowry gift. Most important, it has been made with love. The daughters gaze at it wistfully and wonder whether they will ever own such a beautiful ornament. Their father can make all sorts of things out of bamboo – baskets and flutes and bows and arrows – but he is no silversmith.

The eldest daughter looks covetously at the gleaming silver. At 14, she is almost old enough to begin courting and is looking forward to joining in the "song talk" at New Year. She has a quick brain and a lively tongue and is sure to be a big success at singing clever retorts to her suitors. But so far she has managed to collect very few silver pieces and somehow the excitement of courting will be dimmed if she cannot dress as brilliantly as she can sing.

Her father, pausing in doorway, can almost read these thoughts and he puzzles to know how to help her. The family has been getting poorer and poorer over the last year. He sacrificed all their pigs and chickens to propitiate the spirits when his mother was ill, and then went heavily into debt to buy more to sacrifice for the spirits at her funeral. And then the opium crop was very poor this year and there was no money for anyone in the village. Fortunately the rice is growing well so no one has gone hungry — yet. But a man must help his daughter to attract a suitor. Perhaps he could sell his silver pipe to a tourist in town, but he will have a bitter fight with his father and hear again the arguments — all true, no doubt — about losing independence, pride and dignity. But the old man refuses to admit the importance of that other need, security. A man must take care of his family.

Grandfather simply denies that any changes are necessary. He won't believe that opium is no longer dependable as a source of cash and just snorts when new ways of earning money are discussed.

The old man still thinks you can move any time, anywhere. But today there are many bitter land arguments raging among the tribes as well as with the lowlanders.

He won't listen if anyone tries to tell him that the village can't move on, the way it used to. If you tell him that there are already villages in every promising spot, that a lot of streams are now dry even in the rainy season, and that lowlanders are starting to move into the foothills, he shakes his head in disbelief. He dampens everyone's enthusiasm for trying new crops by insisting that they won't grow, they'll offend the powerful spirits of the fields, that no one will buy them if they do grow, and that they are unsuitable for the villagers to eat because they taste funny.

He ridicules anyone who even considers new methods such as crop rotation or using fertiliser — and his tongue is so sharp! Nor will he concede that the children ought to learn about the country in which the tribe now lives — and will go on living ! — or about the modern world which is no longer avoidable. He doesn't seem to understand that they must learn about these things if they are going to survive. The old days of living in the hills, undisturbed, are over and somehow the tribe will have to adapt, no matter what objections Grandfather might raise.

Father sighs. Then his eyes light on the crossbow, resting on the platform above the fire, and his face brightens. Now there's a possibility! A hunt can earn money if you are careful to choose the right game. The Chinese merchants pay well for bear galls and his family hasn't tasted venison for a long time. But we can't afford to be too choosy these days, for the animals are becoming noticeably scarcer. Any meat will do. Grandfather won't have a single objection to such a traditional pastime. The perfect solution! Temporary, of course, but a solution all the same. He seizes his bow, well-tempered from its months in the smoky atmosphere. Some tobacco, some rice and a small bamboo tube of salt in a shoulder bag complete his preparations, and without a word to his wife, he strides from the house to find some companions to make up a hunting party.

Hilltribes Past and Present

FAAM KAH and his sister Faam Tah created the world. Faam Tah created a huge earth with room for many people, but Faam Kah was lazy and made the sky too small, so his sister had to take her needle and sew the land into hills and mountains to make it fit. Soon there came a great flood and Faam Tah and Faam Kah were only saved by floating to the top of a mountain in a hollowed-out gourd.

At last they decided to marry and after a three-year pregnancy Faam Tah gave birth to a pumpkin. They hurled the pumpkin against the mountain and when it burst its seeds scattered. The few that fell on the mountains became the hilltribe peoples; the many that fell in the valleys became the lowland peoples – greater in number but lower in quality.

This is a legend Yao parents like to recount to their children. Each tribal group has its own version. The Meo, for instance, believe in a brother and sister who gave birth to a piece of meat which subsequently grew into men and women. The Lahu tell of a giant wasp that carried the meat of a dead bull into its hive and "hatched" it into the first man. And every story includes mention of a great flood.

Precise details of the origins of Thailand's hilltribes are still the subject of a considerable research. There are eight major ethnic groups located in northern Thailand, some of them recent arrivals, and all of them part of larger tribal groups scattered through the mountainous area that stretches from Vietnam to Tibet, and north into China. A possible exception is the Lawa or Lua group who claim to have been located exclusively in Thailand for over 900 years. They are probably related to the Wa of Burma who believe their ancestors migrated through Thailand. These people are of Austronesian stock, with slightly negroid features, and their origins are probably in the south, though their exact ethnic affiliations are unclear. Some of the Lawa say their ancestors were chased into the mountains by a huge rolling stone. The great stone lost track of them but it still sits waiting — and they point out an enormous rock in the small river valley of Mae La Noi.[1] None of the Lawa people will ever speak in the Lawa dialect while in its vicinity, fearing that it will recognise their distinctive Mon-Khmer tongue and start chasing them again.[2]

The other seven ethnic groups have migrated south to the present locations in Thailand. Strong Chinese influence is still evident among the Meo, who are mentioned in ancient Chinese chronicles as living in Kiangsi and Hunan provinces. After centuries of conflict they were eventually driven south into the mountains of Kweichow province, and have subsequently scattered even further south through Tonkin, Burma and Laos. Over the last hundred years approximately 30,519 have settled in Thailand.[3] Their exact location is difficult to pinpoint because they move fairly regularly around the triangle formed by Tak, Chiang Mai and Nan. Recently they have started migrating south into Kamphaeng Phet. Another Meo group has recently settled in the northeast near Loey, having migrated to Thailand to escape the fighting in their home area of northern Laos. Although they have intermarried extensively with the Chinese, they remain a distinct linguistic and racial group which recognises two major sub-groups within the tribe — the Blue and the White.

The Yao also trace their origins to China. Their existence was recorded in central China as early as 2500 B.C. According to their traditional legends, the Yao descended from a dog. Once upon a time a dog obliged a Chinese emperor by killing a bothersome enemy. As a reward, the emperor gave the dog his daughter in marriage. This unusual couple settled in the mountain regions of southern China, and their descendants became the Yao tribes of today.[4] There are an estimated four million Yao in Vietnam, Laos, Thailand and the Chinese provinces of Kwangsi and Yunnan. About 21,074 live in Thailand. The first Yao groups moved into Thailand from Laos about 100 years ago. Most of them, however, still consider China to be their true homeland and centuries of intermarriage with the Chinese have given them fair complexions and Mongolian features.

The Karen people live mainly on the northern and western borders of Thailand. There are 175,616 of them, descendants of Karens who migrated from Burma several generations ago. Their legends say they used to live in Thailand hundreds of years ago when it was ruled by the Mon-Khmer — before the Thais came. It is difficult to trace their origins with any certainty and they remain perhaps the most puzzling of the hilltribes because of their apparent lack of relationship to everyone else. The tribe has several subdivisions, but the two major groups in Thailand are the Sgaw and the Pwo. These groups are physically and culturally distinct, and together make up the largest hilltribe group in Thailand. They regard themselves as the first and eldest people and consider all outsiders to be "younger brothers".

A very small group of Kayah live in the Mae Hong Son area. Although there are many of these people in Burma, there are only about 10 tiny villages in Thailand. They appear to be linguistically and culturally distinct from all the other tribes.

The other three tribes — Akha, Lisu and Lahu — have a linguistic relationship to one another. They are all of the Tibeto-Burman group and are believed to have come from the ancient Lo-Lo tribe that once maintained independent kingdoms in the border areas of Yunnan and Szechwan provinces in China.

There are only about 17,000 Lahu in Thailand, and most of them have migrated from Burma only within the last 80 years. The Lahu Na are considered the "great" or "root stock" Lahu by members of the tribe, but there are very few of them in Thailand. The Lahu Nyi are the largest group, followed by the Lahu Shehleh and the Lahu Shi. Their villages are scattered in the Chiang Mai — Chiang Rai — Mae Hong Son triangle.

A small group of Lahu Shi, or Lahu Si as they call themselves, migrated through Thailand in the 1890s, and most of them ultimately settled in the hills of Laos. Recent political events in Laos forced them off their lands, and in 1976 they migrated to Thailand. They are now located in the Chieng Khong refugee camp, where they proudly dressed up in their traditional finery to be photographed for this book. Further research revealed they are closely related to the Lahu Shi village of Ja Pue in the Mae Chan area. To confirm this group's origin, the Thai Hill-Crafts Foundation took a member of Ja Pue village to meet the refugees. There was great excitement as information was exchanged and old relationships brought up-to-date.

The village of Ja Pue is a good example of what happens to small groups living in isolation from others of the same tribe. Ja Pue is located close to a Lisu village, and the men have adopted Lisu dress, retaining only their distinctive Lahu trimmings. The women of Ja Pue have been influenced by the Lahu Nyi, though they have retained the white band on the lower part of their skirts. The jewelry they wear and the household utensils they use are similar to those of the Akha. Recently, a Yao village has

Karen lacquered bamboo basket used for clothes storage. Fine basketwork like this is hard to find today.

located nearby, so the future will likely see a Yao influence in the village as well. The Lahu Shi are a soft, gentle people and not so strongly culture-minded as the Yao and the Meo; therefore they have few compunctions about borrowing whatever elements of hilltribe style appeal to them. In any case, there are few Lahu Shi villages left: no more than five, in Fang and Mae Chan districts.

There are about 10,152 Akha, most of whom have come from Burma and remain located in the far north around Chiang Rai. International boundaries have so little meaning to these people that one village is located in Thailand with some of its fields in Burma! The majority of Akha villages are very poor.

Some studies divide the Akha into 10 to 20 groups according to their clan names. For the purpose of this book, they can be divided into three distinct groups according to their costumes. The Yer Tung Kha (Kha means Akha) come from Shan State, where most of their villages are still located. Some groups of Yer Tung moved into Thailand in the early 1970s. Since they are the latest arrivals, their costumes are still rich in colour, design and accessories, and they wear a great deal of jewelry. The Yer Tung live around Doi Tung near Mae Sai.

The Ya Khong Kha come from the upper part of Shan State and moved into Thailand in the 1930s. Most of them have settled in Pa Mee village near Mae Sai. Their dialect is almost the same as that of the Yer Tung, but the women's headdresses differ slightly.

The Gue Ba Kha are from the southern part of Shan State, and were the first Akha group to move into Thailand. They arrived in the early 1920s. Their villages are located in the Mae Chan area and further south near Mae Suai. Their costumes are comparatively plain as they gradually lose their embroidery designs and colourful trimmings of the costumes of several generations ago. The Gue Ba are the poorest of the Akha. Intermarriage among these three groups is very common.

The Lisu number about 11,260 in Thailand, and are found mostly in villages in the north between Chiang Rai and Mae Hong Son, though some villages are scattered as far as Tak in the southwest and Pitsanulok in the southeast. They are a proud and warlike tribe who have always asserted their independence fiercely. They say that when they found themselves living beside the Chinese after the Great Flood, there was a big argument over who should rule. To settle the matter they decided that the Lisu leader and the Chinese leader should each plant a rod in the jungle, and the owner of whichever rod flowered first should be the ruler. After the rods were planted, everyone slept, but the Chinese leader made sure he woke very early the next day, and when he saw the Lisu rod flowering he quickly exchanged it for his own. Only by this trickery, say the Lisu stories, did the Chinese come to rule the Lisu. According to history, the Lisu always·revolted against any attempts at oppression and in recognition of their bravery these tribesmen were often recruited as government soldiers in ancient China.[5] In a more modern setting, Lisu battalions distinguished themselves in Mesopotamia during World War One.[6] These people have only appeared in Thailand over the last 50 years, most of them having moved from southern China by way of the Shan State in Burma.

All these tribes, then, are known to have ancient origins, and it is possible to follow some of their movements over the centuries. However the nature of their relationship to each other, and to some of the civilisations — such as the Mon-Khmer — that have emerged, flourished and disappeared in the churning turmoil of Asian history remains for the most part a matter for speculation. Linguistic studies seem to offer the most promising clues for discovering such relationships, but most of the languages are so dissimilar that work is slow and difficult. The problem is complicated by the fact that there are no ancient written forms for the languages[7]. There are various stories to account for this, which suggest that at least some of the tribes once had a written language but somehow lost it. The Yao believe their ancestors became so hungry during a great famine that they boiled and ate all their books, and thus lost all record of their writing. The Lisu say they once had a written language but they wrote on skins and the dogs ate them. The Lahu tell a story about how the people of all tribes were called together to receive the teachings of the great spirit. One group took a buffalo skin to write on (the

The fragrant orchid Dendrobidum scabrilingue *which was once offered annually to the ruler of Chiang Mai as a token of loyalty. It is now in danger of extinction.*

Lisu perhaps?) and another took a palm leaf, and the Lisu took a rice cake. On their way home they were so hungry they ate the rice cake and ever since then they have eaten rice pounded with sesame and formed into cakes at New Year to remind them they have God's word in their stomachs. The Meo believe their books were eaten by their horses while they slept, exhausted, after fleeing from the Chinese.

The similarity of these stories, with their insistence that their books were eaten, suggests an attempt to account for what they are coming to see as a deficiency in their cultures. By claiming they have instead a "well-digested" inherent understanding, they are able to justify their customs and traditions.

Whatever relationships there may have been over the past centuries, however, these tribes today consider themselves separate entities. Their languages, customs, beliefs and crafts have developed independently and are generally so distinctive that one tribe is seldom confused with another, even by an outsider. However as movement through the mountain regions becomes increasingly restricted — whether because of war or lack of land or population pressure or stricter control of borders — large numbers of hilltribe people are becoming more settled. Some groups are being resettled into permanent villages, and often find that their nearest neighbours are people from other tribes as well as lowland Thais. Suddenly three or four tribes may find themselves living side by side, and inevitably an interchange of cultures begins. Already the distinctions are blurring; one of the aims of this book is to record the styles of the traditional crafts before they become so intermingled that tribal individuality is lost.

When people are forced to discard a thousand years of history, they become listless and dispirited. The quality of the handicrafts the tribespeople produce today is often not the same as it was a generation ago when they stitched, wove, dyed and carved for the sheer love of it, in the security of their own villages. If outsiders can come to know how difficult it is to produce these traditional handicrafts, they will be able to better appreciate the hilltribe culture.

This book is a record, not of everything, but of what is superb. In this way, it is hoped that it will serve as an inspiration to the hilltribes themselves, and to encourage them continue practising their ancient, beautiful handicrafts.

HILLTRIBE NAMES

Naming the hilltribes can be a confusing and misleading business. Anthropologists and ethnologists have not yet agreed upon a single system of nomenclature, and this creates havoc, especially in the matter of names for subgroups within a tribe.

Akha silver water container and teapot. The Akha are now too poor to buy these.

Metal opium weight used by several of the tribes. (right)

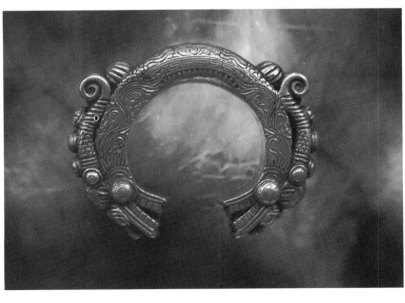

Detail of a sword-handle found in a Meo village. It is carved from an elephant tusk (middle). Carved wooden case for carrying opium balance scale. It depicts a bird carrying a flower. Bird's eye is a red seed (above). Meo man's dragon bracelet of solid silver. This type of work is no longer done by Meo silversmiths (left).

35

Tai-Ya jacket detail.

Example of a lost art (opposite page): Tai-Ya woman's jacket with silver beads. This group has completely stopped dressing in its traditional costumes.

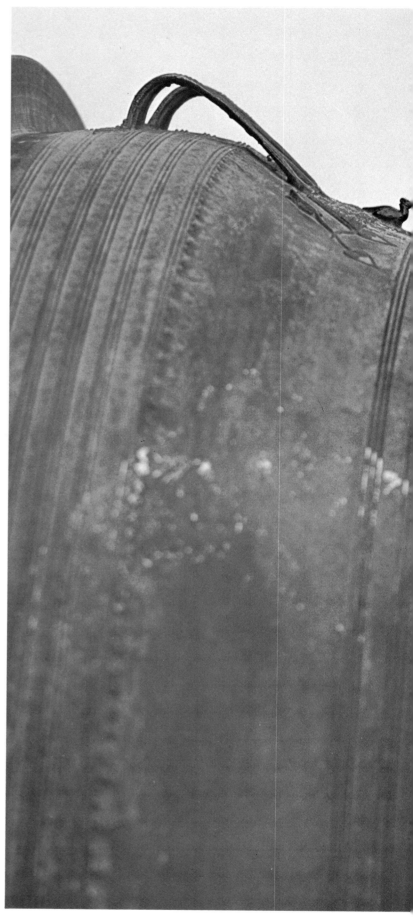

Bronze drum found in a Karen village. In former times, no Karen was considered rich unless he owned one. These drums have an average diameter of 28 cm; height varies from 10 to 50 cm. Detail of drum. From left to right: bird, duck, pig, horse, cow, water buffalo, three elephants separated by conical snails and an unidentified insect.

Thai people generally categorise the tribes by the predominant colour of the women's clothing. Even this is not an infallible rule: The Red Meo, for example, are so called because of their allegiance to the Communists. And the same group of Karen may be called White Karen (for the predominant colour of the unmarried woman's dress) or Red Karen (for the predominant colour of the married woman's costume).

As a general rule, most tribal groups answer to the names used by others, no matter how irrelevant. For example, Thai people refer to the Lahu Shehleh as Muser Dum (Black Lahu) because of their black clothing. However, the group known to the Thais as Muser Krit refer to themselves in their own language as Lahu Na, or Black Lahu — in spite of the fact that Lahu Na costumes include other colours. Similarly, the group known to the Thais as "Blue Meo" refer to themselves in their own language as "Green Meo".

Yao dieties on paper scroll.

The northern Thais use a completely different system in naming the Karen, who have lived in the area for many generations and who are among the most populous of the tribes. This system identifies the Karen groups according to the locations of their established villages. Thus, Yaang Galer Hoong are Sgaw Karen living near swampy lowlands, and Yaang Galer Doi are Sgaw Karen living in mountainous areas. Yaang Pieng are Karen living in the lowlands at the foot of a mountain, while Yaang Doh Dae are those living near a river. And as if things weren't confusing enough, the Yaang Baan (Village Karen) are those who live in the jungle, while the Yaang Pa (Jungle Karen) are those living in areas near lowland towns!

Northern Thais use the general term *Khae* to refer to other tribes. *Khae* could mean Meo, Yao, Lisu and sometimes a Yunnanese. In remote areas the hilltribes are often referred to as *Maeng* (insects), not in a derogatory way, but simply to differentiate them from the lowlanders, who have different customs.

Interpretation of the names also differs. If you ask a Lahu Gui tribesman what Gui means, he might say it is because his group ate *gluay* (bananas) during a famine, while someone from the same village might tell you it comes from *guoy,* a woven back pack which is used by his people.

Because this book is concerned with handicrafts, we have omitted sub-groups of tribes which have stopped making and using their traditional crafts. The Gua M'ba Meo, for example, are very few in number and have been assimilated into other Meo groups. Similarly, a separate group known as the Tai-Ya, which moved into Thailand about 1930, has completely stopped making handicrafts and will therefore not be considered in this book.

For this book, we have chosen the most popular nomenclature, whether technically correct or not. The following chart should help to iron out any ambiguities.

Common English Name	What Thai People Call Them	What they call Themselves
Akha	E-Gaw	Akha
Kayah	Yaang Daeng	Kayeh
Pwo Karen	Yaang Daeng	Plong
Sgaw Karen	Yaang Garieng or Garieng	Phga-ganyaw
Lahu Na (Black Lahu)	Muser Krit (from Christian)	Lahu Na
Lahu Nyi (Red Lahu)	Muser Daeng	Lahu Nyi
Lahu Shehleh	Muser Dum	Lahu Shehleh
Lahu Shi (Yellow Lahu)	Muser Gui	Lahu Si
Blue Meo	Meo Lai	H'moong Njua
White Meo	Mei Khao	H'moong Dher
Yao	Yao	Mien

The Function of Craft

Knives for slitting opium poppy pods and
curved scraper for collecting resin.

Making articles by hand has always been a necessity for the hilltribes. Although they have been able to earn some cash by growing opium, the income involved has never been large, for it is not the grower who makes the great profits in any drug trade. And of course not all tribal people grow it. Money earned by other means — such as selling food crops and jungle products — is even smaller in amount and often less certain. Yet money is necessary to buy essentials such as pots, salt, knives (and more recently, guns), and that greatly desired luxury, silver. Some groups also buy cloth, notably the Yao. A very small cash income has to stretch a long way, so wherever possible everything else is made. The women are responsible for all clothing, including blankets and bags, while the men produce the baskets, weapons, traps, tools, musical instruments, and work the silver.

Despite this apparent sharing of craft work, hilltribe women actually work much harder than their men, both at the crafts and as a general pattern of their existence. The textile crafts require months of work, often beginning with the growing and harvesting of cotton or hemp, then the necessary spinning, weaving and dyeing, and of course the time-consuming decoration of the garments. The women are also responsible for caring for the children, planting, weeding and harvesting the food crops, cooking, cleaning, and tending the animals. They rise before dawn and labour all day, yet somehow manage to find time to do finely detailed craft work all year round.

The men not only have far more leisure, but the crafts for which they are responsible are only occasionally required — houses are re-thatched only once every two years, for instance, and a crossbow, trap or storage basket usually lasts several years. Silver is produced regularly, but there are very few smiths — perhaps one in every 10 or so villages.

There has been little interest in the "larger" crafts such as furniture building or house decoration, or in the "breakable" ones such as pottery, because most of these tribes are migratory, farming by a slash-and-burn method and moving on as soon as the land is exhausted. Everything must be worn or carried — or abandoned — when the tribe moves. Houses, therefore, are simple wood and bamboo structures intended to give adequate shelter for a few years but offering little in the way of comfort or beauty. Furniture is minimal and made of rattan and woven bamboo, light to carry or easy to replace.

The few examples of large crafts to be found in the hilltribe villages are usually made of wood, and their importance is linked to their position, so it is not necessary to move them when the village is vacated. Rice pounders, animal troughs and large water containers are carved out of tree trunks in most villages, and sometimes wood is also used to shingle a roof.

The Akha erect a large wooden gateway over the path to the village, intending it as a barrier to all evil spirits. Crudely carved wooden figures of men and women are grouped around the base of the gate to ensure the fertility of the tribe, and the protection and well-being of the village is renewed every New Year with the erection of a new gate. The number of years an Akha village has remained in one place can be easily seen from the number of gates it has.

The Akha also use wood to make their New Year swings. Tree trunks set into the ground form the framework of the two types of swings. Four trunks support a rope loop swing, while two trunks supporting a crosspiece are the basis of another swing which looks a little like a ferris wheel. The swinging ceremony is the centre of festivities at an Akha New Year, and they believe it was ordered by the gods to ensure a good harvest[9].

The Lawa set up two carved wooden posts in each village where the spirits of their ancestors or the guardian spirits of the village are believed to live, and around these posts all important sacrifices take place. In former times, there was only one post. Then an evil spirit sent an arrow into the post, splitting it in two. Not knowing which half was inhabited by the spirit, the Lawa decided to keep both just to be on the safe side, and this custom has persisted to the present. The oldest of the posts is replaced periodically whenever the shaman decides it is time for a new one.

The Lawa sometimes carve an elaborate lintel from wood which is placed over the main entrance to the house. Not all houses have this decoration, for it contains an element of risk. It may confer great good fortune on the household, but if it is set unevenly or the carving is less than perfect, it can bring ill fortune. They also show an appreciation of shape and texture in their building materials, weaving alternate strips of rough and shiny bamboo for the walls of their houses. This interest in house decoration, unusual among the hilltribes can perhaps be accounted for by the fact that the Lawa practise crop rotation and do not migrate.

Other hilltribe people do not have strong feelings for their homes, as evidenced by the fact that no hilltribe language has separate words for house and home. All houses within the same tribe look pretty much alike, and decoration is generally limited to bundles of herbs drying over the hearth. When a tribesman returns to his house, he is generally too tired to do more than sit and gaze into his hearth fire.

For the tribespeople, the whole village is home. When a tribesman says he is homesick, he means that he misses the ambience of his village, with the children playing in the streets and his family around him. In each village there is a shaman who is the main hope when trouble — bad luck, illness — strikes. When tribespeople move to the lowlands, their homesickness is for the hills where the shaman can perform his comforting rites. But they never miss a particular structure.

Perhaps as compensation for the plainness of their dwellings, hilltribe clothes are extremely elaborate. Various tribes weave, tie-dye, batik and applique cloth, and garments may be decorated with embroidery, tassels, seeds, pompoms, and of course silver ornaments. Everything except the silver is made by the women and in several of the tribes the fineness of a woman's work determines not only her status in the village but also her desirability as a bride. Crafts are used, then, to establish a kind of female social hierarchy within each village.

Traditional Akha house architecture.

Tree trunk used as water container in a Meo village.

They also function as economic indicators. A woman who uses market-bought cloth rather than homespun, who buys chemical dyes rather than making her own, and who can take the time to prepare the most intricate of the traditional patterns is signalling her economic status among her fellows. The most obvious economic indicator, of course, is silver. This is the main form of wealth in the hills and represents a woman's dowry, a man's bank account, a family's savings and everyone's insurance against hard times. At New Year every piece of silver is worn, partly because this is when everyone wants to look his best and partly as a demonstration of affluence.

Surprisingly few of the crafts have any religious significance. Although the tribes are animists and believe in spirits which inhabit the stones, streams, trees and hills of their environment, their main concern is to remain unnoticed by these spirits. Religious ceremonies are therefore concerned mainly with propitiating a spirit which for some reason has become malevolent, and animal sacrifices are the usual solution to such a problem.

Some families maintain a small "spirit shelf" in their homes on which food is offered in tiny cups of Chinese porcelain or fashioned from bamboo. The Meo decorate these altars with cut-outs made from bamboo paper. The Lahu sometimes use strips of bamboo to build small altars outside the village dedicated to spirits that must be encountered regularly; these are adorned with star-like symbols, woven from pieces of bamboo. Similar signs are seen on Akha spirit gates and on newly-built Yao houses. In each case, they are intended to discourage any evil intentions of the spirits. They are sometimes used to indicate that outsiders must stay out of the village in which a ceremony is in progress. The Yao also carve a wooden "stamp" with which to print the spirit money and "passport to heaven" which their priest burn at funerals. Most of these religious articles, however, are simple in design and involve none of the skill devoted to secular crafts.

Of the beautiful textile crafts, only one appears to have an inherent religious purpose. This is the child's hat, worn by every Yao from babyhood to adolescence. It is intended to proclaim him to the spirits as a child of the Yao tribe, who, if he dies, is entitled to be taken to the garden of the spirit world and left to play among the flowers and the butterflies. Even this is only a means of identification. There appears to be no use of most of the crafts as a means of worship or a plea for protection. Some Meo wear a silver lock on their necklaces to protect them from evil spirits, and sometimes purchased amulets and charms are worn for the same reason. Karen women who have had many children die in infancy are believed to be possessed by the soul of a tiger and wear a tiger's tooth to rectify this. Some bracelets and anklets are also connected to spirit worship. But considering the wide range of skills and the large number of crafts the hilltribes produce, religious interests are meagerly served.

Yao ceremonial knife (sui gim) *believed to drive away evil spirits.*

Male and female wooden fertility figures placed next to Akha gates.

Mud puey, *a wooden stamp carved with figures of bird, dragon, tiger and horse. Paper stamped with these figures is burned as a means of sending messages to the gods.*

The head shaman (holding book) leads the initiates up a ladder of "swords". The white cloth represents the pathway to heaven. His assistant is in foreground.

At the culmination of the ceremony, the initiates climb to a wooden platform.

The head shaman throws wooden spirit stamps (ian) *to initiates and their wives, who must receive them in their aprons.*

Dancing at a Yao "initiation" ceremony.
After participating in this ceremony, the initiate
receives a "passport to heaven" which signifies
his ability to communicate more directly with the gods.
He may, if he wishes, become a shaman. This is the most
elaborate and important of the Hilltribe ceremonies,
lasting seven days and nights.

Woman wears a white shoulder band and a yellow tag to identify herself as the wife of one of the initiates

49

The last Hilltribe potter, in the Lawa village of Chang Moh.

Jars for rice whiskey found in a Kayah village.

Akha village gate, called Dto-ma-lok-kong *in the Akha tongue.*

Carved wooden lintel in doorway of Lawa house.

Galeh, or gable, on Lawa house.

Kayah New Year post.

53

Lahu Shehleh dancing pen.

A Meo communal stone grain mill (top left).

Drum in a Haw-yeh, *or Lahu Nyi temple (middle left).*

Akha New Year swing and wheel (left).

Sagang *poles in a Lawa village house the* Pee Sapait,
*guardian spirits who protect the inhabitants, animals and
plantations. They are two to three metres high.*

Lawa foot-operated rice pounder.

Jacket with applique cross to lengthen the life of the wearer.

Pwo Karen hand rice pounder.

A LAHU NYI BLESSING

An elderly villager will be invited to bind the wrists of every newborn baby with cotton string. The strings are thought to protect the baby from misfortune and misery. While performing the binding ceremony, she will deliver this blessing:

> *I tie you with this string*
> *The life string, the immortal string.*
> *May you have merit*
> *May you grow tall and grow fast.*
> *May you be physically strong and quick to learn.*
> *If you look for silver, may you get it.*
> *If you look for gold, may you get it.*
> *May these strings protect you from all sickness.*

Many of the crafts do serve a ceremonial purpose, however. Childbirth among the Meo is the occasion for making an intricate batik-and-applique baby carrier. When they go courting, Lisu men wear elaborate shoulder bags, while Akha men like to carry an ornate silver pipe and silver tobacco box. A number of special crafts are reserved for wedding ceremonies, notably the silver crown of the Yao man, the enormous headdress of his bride, and the paper-thin silver flowers they receive as wedding gifts. As they approach middle age, Meo women begin making jackets with layers of applique on the sleeves for themselves and their husbands to be buried in. These are never stitched together but kept in sections so that they can easily be put on the body.

Pwo Karen girls wear shimmering "singing shawls" to funerals, while the Lawa family wraps its dead in curiously pale-coloured burial blankets.

Both the Karen and the Lawa have brown, glazed pottery jars which have been handed down as the most precious of heirlooms for centuries. The rice whiskey for the spirits is kept in these jars, and to possess one is to possess great status. It is not clear where these jars were made.

Among the Lawa there is still one potter in the village of Chang Moh (Potter's Village), near Mae Sariang, who makes cooking pots and serving bowls of local clay. He sells them in all the villages in the area, his prices are low, but his pots are unglazed and therefore fragile, and so most people prefer plastic and aluminium goods from the market. This potter is the last man to practise what was once probably a common Lawa craft, and his knowledge will die with him, for he has no apprentices.

The focal point for all the crafts, with the exception of bamboo work, is the New Year ceremonies. The Lahu believe if they enter the new year wearing old clothes, their poverty will continue throughout the year[10] and therefore they make a great effort to ensure that every member of the family has a complete set of new clothes for the occasion.

The other tribes seem to share this belief and as a result there is a regular renewal of all textile crafts.

Silver, too, is renewed regularly, though not necessarily each year. A family increases its silver collection whenever there is a little extra money.

Although there are strong traditions of style and decoration in every tribe, a woman may improvise, and often earns great respect if she can think up a new design — provided, of course, that it remains within the framework of tribal taste and does not deviate too far from traditional patterns. Pleasure for maker and beholder seems to be the main principle involved. These factors insure that the crafts remain fluid and constantly revitalised.

The crafts are also playing an increasingly important role as a source of income. Opium is becoming less reliable as a cash crop. As tribal movement is being curtailed, the tribesman faces the problem of coaxing exhausted land to continue growing crops, and for most this involves learning a whole new system of agriculture. In the process, food is scarce.

The discovery that outsiders are prepared to pay for their crafts offers at least a partial stop-gap answer to the hilltribes' predicament. There is probably a psychological as well as a cash value involved here, for at a time of hardship and change within the tribes, with the inevitable insecurity and loss of confidence in old values, the increasing popularity of their crafts must offer some solace.

The crafts also continue to have an extremely important role to play in creating and maintaining a sense of tribal identity. There is tremendous pride in being not only Yao or Meo, but Yao or Meo from a certain village in a certain area. Ways of tying the turban or stitching the jacket proclaim the wearer's background, and these tiny distinguishing features continue to be included in every costume.

The costume is so important that most tribespeople regard it as a literal representation of themselves. The Karen dress their dead in the deceased's best costume, and hang the second-best costume along with other effects from bamboo branches as part of the pre-cremation display. If a Yao shaman is too old to perform his ceremonial dance, he will give his costume to his assistant, who performs the dance in his stead.

But increasing numbers of tribal people are adopting Thai dress. When the men go to the towns they feel less conspicuous and therefore less vulnerable if their clothes are less distinctive. Most women, however, are still proud to wear their traditional costumes, even in town. Children who attend Thai schools must wear uniforms, and many of them never feel comfortable in their own style of dress after being in school for several years. In these ways, tribal people are being slowly "weaned" from their native dress. But this is part of their struggle for survival rather than a deliberate denial of their heritage. Their traditional costumes remain central to their cultures and the crafts essential to their costumes.

Hilltribe Style

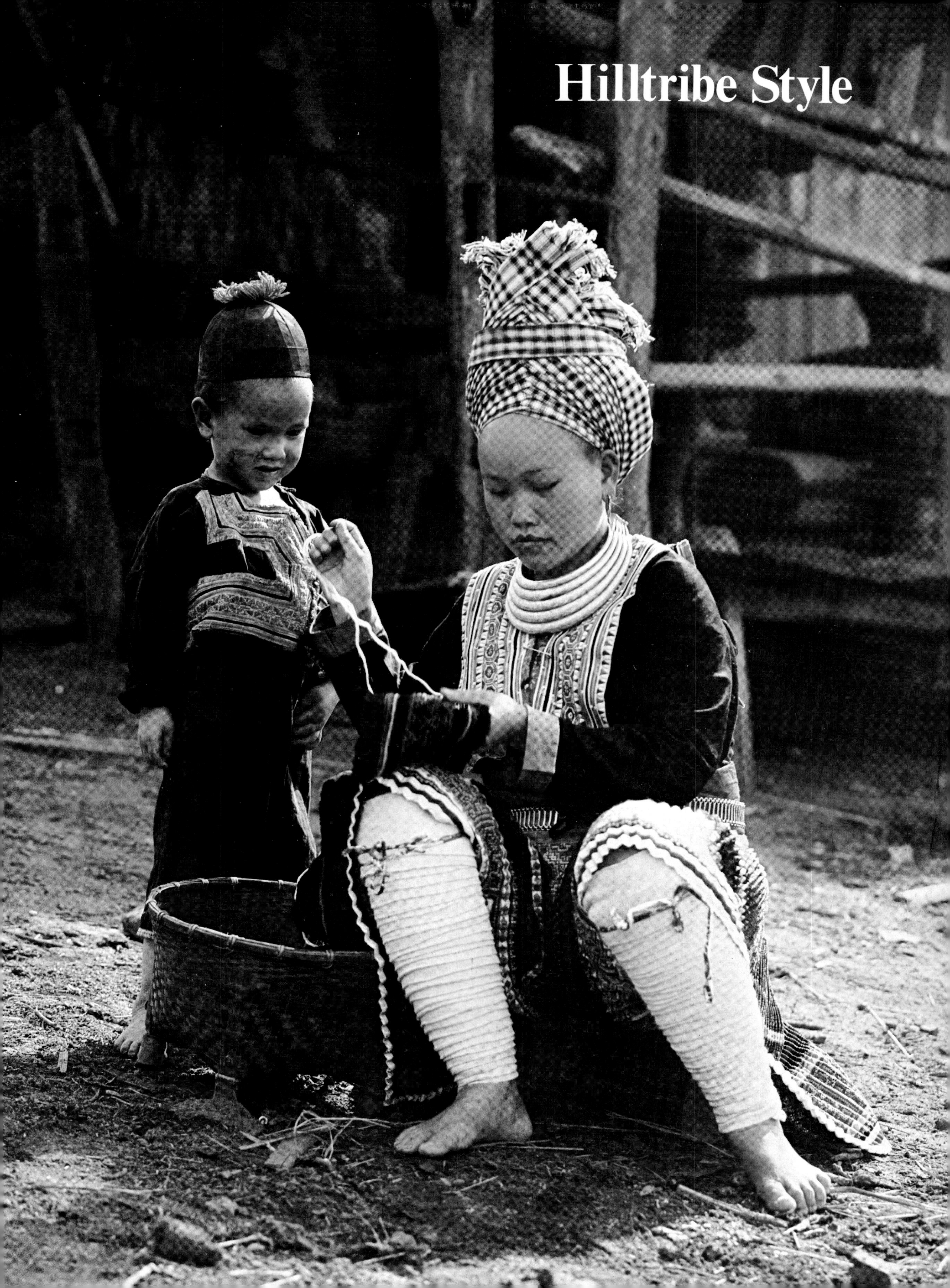

The Akha people say that all their clothes were once indigo. One day a man stole another man's wife and ran off with her. So that she would not be recognised he dressed her in brightly coloured, highly decorated clothes, and since that time the tribe has followed this custom.[11] Soon the new fashion swept the hills. The basic colour of most hilltribe clothes is still indigo, but every group adds its own distinctive decorations.

AKHA

Akha clothes are among the most spectacular in the hills. The women wear intricate headdresses, with a wide variety of decorations. Akha women seldom remove their headdresses, wearing them even when they sleep. They would certainly never appear uncovered in the presence of men or strangers. Their long-sleeved indigo jackets are laden with applique, embroidery, seeds, feathers, buttons and sometimes gibbon fur. On festive occasions the straight edges at the front of the jacket — which usually swing loose — may be held together with large silver buckles.

Their legs are protected from thorns by colourful leggings, and their chests from cold by a narrow breast-band worn under the jacket, covering the breasts and held in place with a single cord. This bodice is mainly for warmth and may be discarded by married women in warm weather, for the Akha, like most of the tribespeople, consider a woman's breasts merely functional once she is married and has a child. An unmarried girl, on the other hand, would be very embarrassed to expose her breasts.

A woman's hips are considered of far greater sexual interest, and their skirts are designed accordingly. They are straight across the front, tightly pleated across the back, slung low on the hips, and reach just above the knee. They wear no undergarments, but a sash weighted with buttons and beads preserves their modesty when they squat and swings alluringly when they walk. This sash is more decorative than functional, for it is worn high on the waist and does not hold the skirt up. It contains a small pocket for holding money, and another on the inside at one end for keeping pieces of cloth to deal with the menstrual flow. Girls of marriageable age often attach a pair of tiny gourds to their sashes so that they will click provocatively with every movement. These are symbolic testicles, a sort of good luck charm to ensure they will get a husband.

In contrast to her everyday wear, an Akha bride appears for the first part of her wedding ceremony in an undyed homespun skirt with an undecorated indigo jacket, her head covered with a wide bamboo and palm leaf hat. Only later will she don an especially elaborate outfit. Similar undyed skirts are worn by the older women of the tribe for their post-menopause "becoming like a man" ceremony, after which they are permitted to take part in religious ceremonies. On each occasion, the white skirt symbolizes an elevation in status.

There are two other occasions when an Akha woman wears white to make her feel special. When she becomes a grandmother, she will don her white skirt and take a sum of money (about $7 US) to her parents. If her parents are dead, she gives the money to her closest relative living in her parent's house. When the buffalo offered at a funeral ceremony is pregnant, the female head of the household puts on her white skirt and takes the fetus away to cook. This is said to bring good luck to the household.

Akha men are far more subdued in their everyday dress. They wear baggy trousers and long-sleeved jackets of plain indigo homespun cotton cloth. The jackets of both men and women have a small open vent below the armpit for ventilation. On festival days, they wear jackets decorated with silver coins, embroidery, applique, feathers and pompoms. It is the custom among the Akha for a girl to ask a boy for a piece of his clothing or jewellery after lovemaking, not only as a love token, but as proof of paternity in case she becomes pregnant. An Akha child must never be born without an acknowledged father.

On important occasions, the men wear headdress consisting of a long tubular piece of cloth, padded and twisted, around the head with the end hanging over the shoulder like a queue. During courting, some men like to decorate these headdresses with flowers and tassels. Both men and women carry shoulder bags adorned with embroidery, buttons, appliqued bands and circles of chicken feathers. The woman's bag has more beads and is smaller than the man's.

Akha men are very particular about how their women dress. No matter how dirty or tatty they themselves are, they will refuse to eat a meal cooked by a woman they consider improperly dressed. And women who wear shoes, or even slippers, are still laughed at.

KAREN

Generally, Karen women wear a sarong-style tubular skirt with horizontal stripes. They bunch the cloth on each hip and tie the skirt in place with string or a strip of cloth. Married women of the Sgaw Karen group appear in skirts of a rusty red colour, with alternate stripes woven from tie-dyed thread. A loose box-shaped black blouse is worn over this and elaborate seed-and-embroidery patterns are worked on the lower border. Among the Pwo Karen group, married women's skirts are usually predominantly brick red, and although their blouses may sometimes be decorated with seeds, there is a trend towards using only bright wools to weave designs into the blouse.

The Karen are found mostly in Mae Saraing, Hot and Chomthong districts. They have many variations in dress because some have been here for many generations, and some arrived only 100 years ago. People who live in these provinces can tell exactly which area a Karen comes from by the variations in the costume.

Pwo Karen young man with traditional hair style.
Blue Meo baby boy's cap.

This is the only tribe which makes a sharp distinction between the clothing of married and unmarried women. Unmarried Karen girls of both groups wear white dresses, the plainness relieved only by red tufted designs woven in at hem and shoulder. In some areas, the lower half of the dress has diagonal tufted designs. They disclaim any symbolism in this insistence on "virginal" white dresses, and maintain that it reflects only a girl's inability to make her clothes any more elaborate while she is young. However, the contrast between the simple shapeless white dress and the straight tight skirt and fancy blouse of the married women certainly suggests to the outside observer the difference between innocence and experience, potential and fulfilment.

The man's shirt is similar in shape to the black blouse of the newly-married woman, but bright red with a few widely-spaced stripes of other colours. Plain black trousers complete the outfit. Some men wear Burmese sarongs instead. As is common with any of the tribes living near large towns, men of both Pwo and Sgaw groups have tended to adopt local Thai dress — that is, western-style shirts and trousers. Pwo Karen men still favour the old style of wearing their hair long, pulled down to one side and knotted, and among men of both groups a nondescript turban (often a towel) is optional.

At home, Pwo Karen men prefer to wear Burmese-style sarongs and white homespun jackets with red embroidery securing the seams. The sarongs consist of four panels, two of plain red material alternating with two of black material with white stripes.

Many of the men are tattooed from waist to knee with dark blue animal designs. Some also have coiling designs on their arms. Although the process is very painful, Karen men believe it is a symbol of manhood.[12] Some Karen women like to tattoo the backs of their hands to ensure dexterity in the manual arts.

KAYAH

Kayah women wear read or black cloth tied across one shoulder and held in place by a long white sash fringed with red. This is wound several times around the waist and tied below the buttocks. A red or black striped sarong-style skirt is worn underneath this, reaching to the knee. Below this, they wear a remarkable style of legging. They begin about the age of five to tie a few strands of lacquered cotton cord around the calf, and over the years they add more and more cord until the leggings reach a depth of about 15 centimetres and a weight of two kilograms each. These must be adjusted every day, but they are seldom removed and the legs of an adult woman are deformed as a result. The story goes that long ago this was done to stop young girls from eloping; it certainly forces women to walk very slowly. Today they say they do it to add strength to their legs in walking long distances and so they can carry heavy loads over very steep hills. In Kayah circles, the bigger the leggings the more fashionable the woman.

When a young couple become engaged they live together until one, or preferably two, children have been born to them. Only then they go through a marriage ceremony. The bride will wear a black striped cloth for her off-shoulder top on this occasion, though any woman may wear the same style at any time. If a woman remains childless, her "fiance" will move out and choose another wife.

The men of this tribe have always been mahouts and have travelled widely with their elephants. As a result, they have lost whatever traditional costume they once had. No one in the tribe even remembers what it once looked like. Today they wear baggy black pants for everyday, and purchase western-style outfits at the market for New Year.

LAHU

The Lahu Na consider themselves the senior members of their tribe, and their costumes have a dignity appropriate to that claim. Traditionally the long skirts of the women were plain black with applique stripes or zigzags in bright colours around the bottom. The modern trend is to weave narrow stripes of colour into the cloth of the whole skirt, with a border of wider stripes at top and bottom. The cloth is only 40 centimetres wide and two pieces must be sewn together horizontally and joined at the ends to make a sarong-style skirt. Lahu women wear their skirts with a fold at the front, and hold them in place with a silver belt or a piece of cord. For everyday use, they wear a short straight black jacket with banded sleeves of red and white. For best effect, they wear a long indigo homespun tunic

The Gue Ba Akha skirt hangs very low.

Pwo Karen man makes offering to rice field spirits.

Akha woman's shoulder bag. The man's bag is the same, but it has no decoration along the bottom edge underneath the banded area.

Pwo Karen shoulder bag.

Sgaw Karen shoulder bag.

Lahu Na shoulder bag with applique.

Lahu Na woven shoulder bag.

Lahu Nyi shoulder bag.

Lawa shoulder bag.

Lisu shoulder bag.

Kayah women at New Year festival (top left). Women may wear black or red according to personal preference.

Pwo Karen wooden clogs used by women during rainy season.

Blue Meo men getting ready to welcome the King of Thailand to their village.

Young Pwo Karen man returning home from rice fields.

Lahu Shi from Mae Chan area.

Akha man with lowland hairstyle but traditional finery (opposite page).

Child wears a dress fashioned from the leg of her father's discarded trousers.

The full Blue Meo costume. Note bamboo hardwood pipe.

Blue Meo bride and groom.

Yao couple returning from their fields. Man carries fodder for his horse; woman carries gourds with the day's water supply.

Lisu youth pass through poppy fields on their way to "song talk" courting ritual at New Year festival.

Lahu Na woman in full costume.

Lahu Shi women in a refugee camp. Women second left and far right are unmarried.

Yer Tung Akha woman models appliqued hood, jacket and shoulder bag.

Yer Tung Akha women.

Yer Tung Akha woman.

A Sgaw Karen bride (in black) with her bridesmaid on a shopping trip the day after the wedding.

White Meo woman in her working clothes.

Kayah woman in her wedding costume and heavy lacquered leggings.

Lahu Shehleh girl (opposite page) has cut her hair short to make it easier to carry heavy loads with a head-strap. Note bands of lowland and printed cloth on her traditional jacket.

Young Lisu girls.

Another style of Lisu New Year costume for men.

Pwo Karen unmarried girl.

*Yao shaman and his assistant. The shaman is reading
from a book of Chinese characters. Note shaman's
moulded tin walking stick.*

with a high neckline and long sleeves, cut diagonally across the breast and fastening down the front or to one side. The edges and front hem are bordered with banding five centimetres wide and back hem is embroidered. A heavy border of silver half-sphere studs and dangling silver ornaments is sewn onto the high collar, across the back, and along the diagonal front opening. Coloured bands decorate the sleeves. A simple turban of black or white completes the dress. The Lahu have traditionally carried appliqued shoulder bags.

Lahu men wear a short, black, long-sleeved jacket that opens down the front or side and, for best, will have an edging of red embroidery and be fastened with silver buttons. A black turban four and a half metres long and 56 centimetres wide is the traditional headdress, which is wound doughnut fashion so that the top of the head is left bare. Special turbans for ceremonial occasions have tasselled ends. The cuffs on the trousers are embroidered, with a predominance of red.

The costume of the Lahu Nyi women is very dissimilar to that of their Black Lahu sisters. Their skirts are made of three pieces, each of which is different. The top section is predominantly red, with pinstripes of other colours — notably black, white, green and gold — woven in. The middle piece is plain, often blue or black, and made of velvet for special occasions, cotton for everyday. The border piece is plain red cotton, 15 to 18 centimetres wide, decorated with chain stitch embroidery.

The women's jackets are made either of plain black cotton cloth or of black or blue velvet, with wide red strips sewn onto sleeves and bodice, giving an impression of broad stripes. Narrow strips of blue and white, and sometimes printed material, complete the sleeves. They are always fully lined, and the popularity of gaudy prints from lowland markets for this purpose sometimes creates unusual effects! Traditionally these jackets were tapered to the waist and made to flare slightly over the hips by inserting gussets at the sides and front. The Lahu Shi still make the flared jackets, but this flattering style has now been replaced among the Red Lahu by the straight seamed look that predominates in the hills. Large silver buckles are used to fasten the jackets down the front and though these buckles are now seen on many hilltribe costumes, the Lahu believe the custom was originally theirs. Though of varying sizes, the buckles are arranged merely according to taste, and have no prescribed order.

Lahu Nyi men wear baggy pants which are usually black but may also be blue or green. They are trimmed at leg and waistband with white, and held in place with a piece of cloth used as a sash. The long-sleeved black jackets hang loose to the top of the trousers, and for festivals are decorated with silver half-sphere studs, sewn in groups of three, and occasionally with embroidery. They cover their heads with black turbans.

The Lahu Shehleh are the second largest group of Lahu in Thailand after the Lahu Nyi, though they are only a small community among the Lahu as a whole. Their costume is plain by comparison with the other groups. Their long black tunics, although similar in style to those of the Lahu Na, are usually decorated only with narrow strips of pale yellow and white cloth. The women of this group wear black trousers reaching to mid-calf and both the trousers and the black leggings that protect the lower leg are bound in the same pale colours. The latest trend among this group is to add wide bands of colour to the sleeves, a radical change from the simple elegance of the older style. Some Lahu men wear black trousers with a line of red embroidery at the knee in front, dipping down to the lower edge of the leg in two parallel lines at the back.

In Thailand, the Lahu people often live near Shan villages, and when they choose to discard their traditional costumes they usually adopt Shan dress, especially the Lahu Na. The woman's traditional dress is a short black jacket, flared at the hip and adorned with appliqued bands of bright cloth and some embroidery. Their skirts have three sections. The top panel is made of red pin-striped cloth identical to that used by Red Lahu women. The centre panel is black, decorated with applique, and a bright strip of red, green or blue forms the border. The lower panel is plain white with some trimming at the bottom edge. Perhaps the most noticeable part of the Lahu Shi outfit is the unusual "grey" shoulder bag, although it is now being woven in other colours and is also carried by the other Lahu groups.

LAWA

Lawa dress is perhaps the least colourful of all. The women wear very tight black striped tubular skirts with no fold or pleat, held in place with a silver belt, string, or sometimes just a knot of the cloth. Their blouses are usually white, similar in styling to the Karen ones, but undecorated except for rows of embroidered asterisk shapes along the seams. For wedding Lawa women wear short-sleeved black blouses made from homespun cotton and decorated with silver wire stitched in vertical lines down the front. Their arms are covered to the wrist with tight-fitting sheaths of cloth that fit the blouse sleeve.

Although most of the sarong-style skirts have simple horizontal stripes as their only decoration, some women weave short lengths of cloth with striking "lightning" patterns using tie-dyed thread of dark blue, white and red. Skirts made by sewing these pieces together brighten festival days. Strings of coins and beads, large ivory earrings and rope-like bracelets are the only ornaments of the Lawa women, but they seem inseparable from their curving buffalo horn and silver pipes, so these should perhaps be counted as part of their costume. Their heads are usually left bare and their hair pulled back into a bun. Their shoulder bags are plain and they find the more elaborate bags of other tribes most attractive — and desirable — as a result.

Lawa jackets are always short-sleeved. When they work in the fields, the women add a sleeve and hold it in place with brass bracelets and armbands.

The men have almost completely adopted the dress of the Thai farmers and only their curving pipes now identify them as tribesmen. Traditionally, they dressed in plain white homespun trousers and shirts. A curious addition to the shirt is made by the shaman who puts spirals of red cord front and back. The reason behind these very old designs has now been lost. Lawa men tattoo themselves from waist to knee with designs of tigers and apes as protection against attacks from these animals.[13]

MEO

The costume of the Meo women has a certain stylistic resemblance to that of the Akha, notably in the short pleated skirts. Meo skirts are pleated all the way around, however, and the smaller, closer pleats use considerably more material, making the skirts fuller and heavier. A decorative appliqued apron is worn down the front and tied at the back with red cloth strings that have embroidery and tassels on the ends. It has an even more vital role as a pre-server of decorum than the Akha sash because Meo skirts are not seamed at the front. Because these skirts are very

Lawa Shaman wearing his ceremonial jacket.

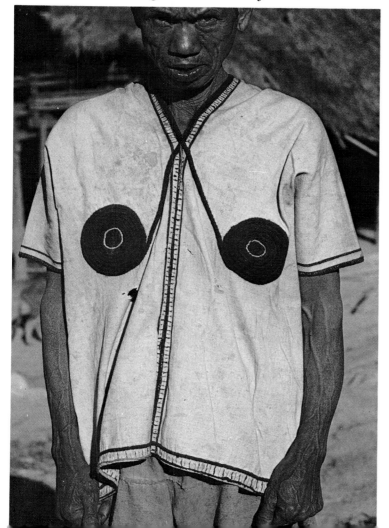

thick, it is easier to wash and dry them if they are left open. In the damp weather of the hills, anything that will speed the drying process is useful. Although the ends of the skirt may overlap a few inches at the waist, they swing apart at the bottom and the apron is essential to cover the gap. The Meo believe that a woman can cure her husband of any illness by dipping her apron in warm water and bathing his face with it.[14] White Meo aprons are indigo with a wide border of blue cloth.

Among the Blue Meo the skirts are dyed indigo with batik patterns, an embroidered border and applique decorations. White Meo skirts are white without any decoration at all. With these skirts they wear short-waisted jackets with applique shapes on the collar and front edges, and on the back (but not the front) hem. Plain leggings complete the outfit. Highly decorated "bibs" are still worn for New Year, but the old custom of wearing white leggings of intricately-wound strips of homespun cloth has almost completely disappeared.

Meo men wear unique trousers. They are cut from two large rectangles of cloth and sewn so that the crotch hangs very low, sometimes only 15 centimetres from the ground. These loose, baggy trousers give the wearer a sense of freedom of movement. They are made of ordinary factory-made material purchased from local traders, undecorated except that the rough edges are oversewn with buttonhole stitch. On gala days, an embroidered sash is worn around the waist, the ends hanging down in front. The long-sleeved jackets are cut short, so that the midriff is usually left bare, and they are closed diagonally across the chest with small silver bell-shaped buttons. Her man's chest is also the favourite place for displaying a woman's supreme efforts in the arts of applique and embroidery, and his best jacket is often a very gaily decorated garment as a result. A sateen skull-cap topped with a pink pompom is traditional headgear, though black turbans are occasionally substituted.

YAO

Yao women always wear pants and concentrate their decorating skills on the embroidery for their trousers. The loose, ankle-length tunic worn over them is left plain black or indigo except for a thick ruff of magenta-coloured wool at the neck, and is split up to the thigh on each side. A small pompom dangles from the top of the split. The embroidered front of the pants is always fully exposed because the women tuck the long front pieces of the tunic up into the six-metre sash that is wound several times around their waists. The embroidered ends of this sash hang down the back of the tunic. For weddings a bride will add a red sash over one shoulder, a white sash over the other. Her attendants will wear one white sash, and leggings made from narrow, embroidered strips. The finishing touch to the everyday outfit is a heavy indigo turban which is also decorated with some embroidery, and without which no Yao woman is ever seen except in the privacy of her home. On festival days, some Yao women wear aprons with silver studs.

Yao men wear the plain indigo pants which seem to be *de rigeur* for Hilltribe men. Their jackets are loose-fitting, cut on the diagonal from left to right across the front, fastening at the neck and hip with silver bell buttons. The women used to embroider patterns across the chest, following the line of the diagonal opening, but styles have changed and modern jackets usually have just one complete pattern beside the hip fastening. The edges of the jackets are usually bound in red and white strips of cloth. Sometimes coiled strips of silver wire embroidery are added between the strips. Men often go bareheaded, although black felt berets are considered highly fashionable and are a popular addition to a Yao man's wardrobe.

The Yao buy their shoulder bags in the market, and add their Yao trademark by stitching on two rows of embroidery at the top opening of the bag and an exuberant display of pompoms.

The Yao shaman wears a brilliant tunic made from Chinese brocade, usually red and blue, held in place with a multi-coloured brocade sash. A black sateen cap and an ivory-topped wooden staff complete his ceremonial outfit. The shaman is literate in Chinese. Though the Yao have no written language of their own, the shamans have transliterated Yao prayers and incantations into Chinese characters, and every shaman has a book from which he will read during ceremonies.

GENERAL REMARKS

In all tribes, children wear small versions of the adult costumes. Young boys and girls often discard the lower parts of their costumes, and in this the boys have the advantage, for they can wear an extra-long blouse and go without underpants.

Both men and women use face powder at festivals. Women like to try on lipstick, especially the Meo, and use it as rouge as well, in Chinese-opera fashion.

When young people of both sexes go courting they like to carry white terrycloth hand towels instead of handkerchiefs. These are printed with Chinese letters and "Good Morning" in English.

Men have several ways of showing their virility. They may expose their stomachs to show strength. The Akha jacket is slit up the back to expose the wearer's strong back muscles. Tattoos, too, are a sign of virility — or at least, the wearer's bravery in enduring the pain of the process. And some tribesmen like to wear a band of cloth around their heads to give them a feeling of being ready to go, to work hard.

One slightly confusing aspect of Hilltribe style is the seemingly endless variation in detail that occurs from group to group, and even from village to village in the same group. The Lahu and Karen offer excellent examples of this. Several small groups within these tribes claim a separate identity on the grounds of a tiny but distinctive feature of the dress. The La-Law and Phu Lahu, for instance, broke away from Lahu tradition because they came to believe that good spirits preferred white, and therefore they no longer dye their clothes. The Ku-Lao Lahu, a subdivision of the Lahu Na regarded by some as the elite of the tribe, have symbols of the sun, moon and stars on the sides of the women's jackets, believing the sun signs will give a strong voice in the courting songs, the moon will give the ability to see in the dark, and the stars will give good luck (in the form of good weather) at courting time. This group is also the only one to sew half-sphere studs in a horseshoe pattern to decorate the front of the jacket and to use four silver buckles of diminishing sizes to fasten it.

The pace of fashion change in the hills is very fast now. For one thing, the way of life is changing. The Akha used to grow upland rice, but now they grow wet rice and cannot wear their beautiful leggings to work the fields. Meo ladies who live in the lowlands have been murdered for their silver neck rings, and so have had to stop wearing them.

Material is now easier to get, and in greater variety. In Hot, jackets were once yellow and red. Now shocking pink and green are available as well. Tribespeople who were once dependent on what the traders brought to the village can now choose from the great variety of fabrics and decorations offered in lowland towns, and can experiment. Pwo Karen women are beginning to string plastic buttons together as bracelets and necklaces.

Religion, too, has played its part in changing traditional hilltribe garb. The teaching of both Christian and Buddhist missionaries implies that style of dress and colour are not important, and converts are encouraged to break clothing and colour taboos.

The Thai passion for uniforms has helped to displace Hilltribe costumes. Hilltribe headman must wear their uniforms when they go to meetings in town; schoolchildren must wear uniforms to study in Thai schools.

And finally, time is becoming a factor. For the first time the hilltribes are beginning to acquire a sense of time. Where once an elaborate costume was merely a costume, it is becoming for some a valuable item in terms of manhours. Some tribespeople are beginning to think it's not worth spending endless hours making some of the more intricate items of dress.

But whatever the costume, and whatever the changes, the tribes feel comfortable and attractive in it, and it works for the kind of life they lead.

While the larger stylistic traditions endure — Yao women will continue to wear trousers and Meo women their pleated skirts — the finer points of colour, decoration, and even material belong to the world of fashion that is no more elastic in the hills of Thailand than it is anywhere else.

JANUNG ADJUSTED *his mirror glasses. He was very conscious of being in the height of Lawa fashion because he was wearing them, and he hoped Pa knew it too. He watched her surreptitiously as she brought forward the lacquered tobacco box for her visitor. Her name meant "forest" because that was where she had been born. And it suited her. He thought her smile was as radiant as a glistening forest after the rain.*

He accepted the bamboo box rather haughtily, as custom required, but as she turned demurely away, he called her back.

"There is no tobacco in this."

"But I just filled it this evening," she protested.

"Look and see."

With a small frown she took the box and opened it. Inside, nestled on the tobacco, was a small parcel of betel nut, coins and betel leaves smeared with lime, she blushed furiously. He must have slipped it in after she had given it to him. Now she was caught right in front of him, with nowhere to look but the floor. She gave him a quick nod, handed the box back to him, and fled.

Later, alone, after she had regained her composure, she thought about Janung. He was supposed to be a descendant of Lord Wilanka, a powerful Lawa headman who had been an admirer of Queen Chamtewi of Lampoon. His family was very respected. And he was handsome, too, and gentle. But she had hardly dared hope that he would come courting, that he might ask her to make him a pair of trousers in the old symbolic way. She thought again of the message contained in the tobacco box and again her cheeks flamed.

For the next month she worked steadily at her loom. Every free moment she had she would sit flat on the floor, strap the side belt around her back and set the shuttle flying. She was careful to lean well back to hold the tension steady. The first skirt she had made on this loom was so loosely woven that it bagged and sagged. She had been very self-conscious in it, and had worked long hours to make a replacement in a hurry. But that lesson had been well-learned – this cloth was even and firm, good enough to give to Janung. She went to sleep every night conscious of back muscles sore from sitting upright for so long. But it was worth it.

A moon later, Janung returned. Pa greeted him quietly and dutifully offered him the hospitality of the house – the tobacco box. Janung began to fill his pipe, but suddenly Pa stopped him.

"I nearly forgot – Father brought some special new tobacco back from the market. Would you like to try it? It's on the shelf to the left of the fire."

Janung went to the shelf. This time it was his turn to blush, for instead of tobacco, he found the trousers, smoothly white as expected, but audaciously stitched with black thread. She was very up-to-date. He glanced quickly at Pa and this time she held his look for a moment before lowering her eyes.

She toyed with the flower in her hair. He fiddled with his pipe. The moment was ripe for the proposal.

Cotton is the woman's plant.

Akha women spin thread whenever their hands are free. A visitor to a remote Akha village, such as Saen Sa-Ad, high in the hills south of Chiang Rai, will notice that the trails are littered with small bits of discarded cotton fluff, a sure sign that women have passed that way to and from their work in the mountain rice fields.

Cotton also plays a central role in offerings the Lahu, Lawa and Karen tribespeople make to the spirits. It is used to represent both clothing and white flowers.

Two types of cotton are grown: one with a long white staple, and the other with a much shorter, ochre-coloured staple. The Lawa prefer the latter, which produces a thicker and more nubbly cloth than that of other tribes. It has the added advantage of being warmer.

Home-grown cotton is still a source of thread for weaving homespun cloth, especially in more remote areas. The Akha in particular still prefer to have their own supply, and their women are seldom seen without a small bamboo basket full of cotton tufts and a tiny spindle the size of a crochet hook. The Karen, Lawa and Lahu use a large, hand-operated spinning wheel, while the Meo have a foot-pedal spinning wheel.

A wooden cotton gin with hand-turned rollers is used to remove the seeds. The Akha cover one roller with metal. The Karen gin has a piece of cloth at the top to brush off the seeds. An instrument made of bamboo and string, which looks a little like an archer's bow, is used to "shoot" the cotton and make it into fluffy tufts seven to 10 centimetres long, from which the thread is spun. After that, the thread is rolled onto spools ready for weaving.

The Meo and Lisu use a different fibre to produce cloth. This is a type of hemp, obtained from a plant of the cannabis marijuana family. The stalks are cut, stripped of leaves and dried in the sun for three to five days. The stalks shrink as the excess moisture evaporates. The girls then split the dry stalk into very fine strips, using one long thumb nail grown for this purpose. The fibres are frayed at the ends and folded together, three at a time, into a continuous chain. They hold together even through the process of spinning and boiling in water mixed with ashes, an all-day bleaching process. The resulting coarse white threads are then woven into a heavy cloth which the Meo use mostly for the batik skirts of the women. The Lisu once made all their clothes and blankets with this cloth. The Lisu in Thailand frequently buy their cloth ready-made and when they do weave they like to buy thin cotton thread. Meo women persevere with the production of hemp because it holds pleats better and swings better than cotton cloth — a sort of natural "permapress". The Akha also grow and process hemp, but they use it only to net bags for carrying fish, and to make strings for their crossbows.

There are at least three types of looms used in the hills. The horizontal back-strap loom attaches at one end to a pole in the wall of the house. The weaver fastens the other end around her back with a wide strap made of deer or cow hide and sits on the floor with her legs extended under the loom. A section of bamboo anchored to the floor enables her to brace her feet. The width of cloth woven by this method usually corresponds to the width of the weaver's hips — seldom more than 38 centimeters — and tension is controlled by leaning back against the strap. The Karen use this loom for all their weaving, and it is also used by the Lisu, Lahu, Kayah and Lawa women. The shape of the back-strap looms varies from tribe to tribe, but the principle is the same.

The foot-treadle loom is a large bamboo structure. Four posts are sunk into the ground and rise to a height of nearly two metres. Cross poles are fitted into holes in the uprights and the wooden pieces which support the warp are suspended from these cross pieces on ropes. The whole apparatus is made without using a single nail. The woman stands to operate this loom and uses her feet to work the treadles.

Sgaw Karen skirt length. Pattern comes from tie-dyed thread.

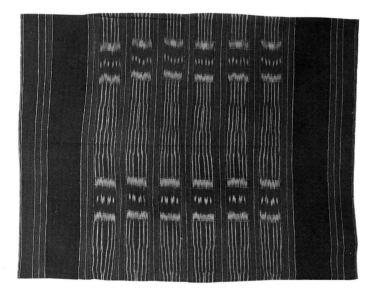

This type of loom is used mainly by the Akha, but sometimes the Lahu Na and Lawa groups use it as well. The cloth from these looms is often as narrow as 20 centimetres and woven very tightly, but the Lahu weave their cloth to widths appropriate to making their two-panelled skirts, anything from 35 to 50 centimetres.

These looms are constructed at the beginning of each dry season just outside the weaver's house, and dismantled at the end of the weaving season. They are easy to make since they are mostly of bamboo.

The Meo have developed an ingenious combination of those two looms. Their loom is attached to a fixed upright structure at one end, but fastens around the weaver's back with a wide strap. The woman usually sits on a wooden bench to operate this loom, and changes the threads with foot pedals. The Lawa sometimes use this type of loom for weaving blankets, though all their clothes are made on a back-strap loom.

Cloth that is to have decoration — such as embroidery or applique — is usually woven from natural-coloured threads and the completed length dyed as one piece. The basic indigo cloth used for much of their clothing is made in this way.

When the colour of the cloth is an integral part of the decoration, however, the thread is usually dyed before weaving. Except for indigo, chemical dyes have almost completely replaced natural dyes and in many cases ready-dyed threads are purchased from traders, eliminating the dyeing process altogether. The Karen and the Lawa are the only tribes to persist with the making of natural dyes other than indigo.

The Sgaw Karen use tie-dyed thread for weaving patterns in the married women's skirts. The secret and time-consuming process of tie-dyeing the threads is described in Chapter 8. Traditionally the pattern consisted of a series of wide stripes of tie-dye, called Crab or Python Skin, separated by one-centimetre stripes of plain red. Today, however, it is easier to use plain threads for the wider stripes and tie-dyed threads for the narrow ones.

The Karen have a legend explaining the origin of the Python Skin pattern. Once upon a time, a Karen woman was abducted by a fabulous white python. It carried her off to its den, and compelled her to weave her clothing in the pattern of its skin. When she was released from the python's den, she showed her contempt for the creature by weaving this design into her sarong. Among the Karen, this is the gravest insult, for a Karen man will never touch or walk under a hanging sarong because of its association with menstruation.

The Sgaw Karen of the Mae Sariang area wear completely different skirts. They weave red and yellow two-centimetre stripes against a background of black, in a strip about 30 centimetres wide. This becomes the centrepiece of the skirt, with strips of cotton cloth sewn horizontally on either side. There are now many variations in the colour and style of the weaving. The people of this area use the same cloth for their shoulder bags.

In the Lawa tribe, one family in every village is skilled in the art of weaving the special burial blankets necessary for the lying-in-state. This is a special skill which always remains the province of one family, who presumably know how to handle the bad spirits associated with death. The dyes used in the tie-dyeing of threads of these blankets produce muted colours which are strikingly different from the strong colours used in other hilltribe articles: grey, blue, pink, pinkish-brown and pale corn yellow.

The blankets are striped, with tie-dyed threads in pink or blue used to weave one-centimetre stripes close to the edges of the blankets. A wide brown stripe down the centre has black zigzag and geometrical shapes woven into it. Two such blankets, of different designs, are required for each funeral, one to go over, one under, the body. This is one of the few hilltribe items that is produced exclusively for ceremonial use.

Lawa women weave their skirts from homespun cotton. The deep blue cloth has horizontal stripes of red and white at top and bottom, and tie-dyed bands of blue and white. In some villages the weavers also like to add a tiny red and yellow stripes. The tie-dyed patterns are called "lightning" designs, and are sometimes woven in red thread instead of blue.[15] The patterns vary slightly from village to village. The large white blouses they wear with these skirts, however, are woven from coarser thread and the design is the same from one village to another.

The Karen are perhaps the most prolific weavers. They are also among the most skilled, for they rely on woven patterns to provide almost the only decoration on their cloth and therefore tend to experiment with colour and design. The articles they produce are all striped, except of course for the white dresses of the unmarried girls and the black blouses of the Sgaw married women. The bands of colour woven into all other articles vary in width from pinstripe size to three centimetres.

They make blankets by weaving three pieces to a length of about two metres and stitching them together. Traditionally these were white with $\frac{1}{4}$-centimetre white stripes, with a border on each edge of the blanket made

Lawa weaver preparing warp.

from two-finger width red stripes. One end was fringed. These blankets are used by the Karen as covers at night, and the fringe must always be at the wearer's feet. Only the dead are covered with the fringe at the top, so it is considered very bad luck to cover oneself with the fringe at one's head. The blankets are also used as baby carriers and slings for carrying many articles. Sometimes white buttons may be sewn all over the blanket in clusters of three or five for decorative purposes. It is the custom in the hills to take along a blanket when visiting overnight, which may help to explain this interest in blanket decoration.

Shorter strips of woven material become shirts, red for men and black for women. Both are made from two rectangular pieces, sewn up front, back and sides, leaving openings for arms and head. Stripes of various colours outline the edges of each piece of cloth in the man's shirt, but the Sgaw Karen woman's blouse material has only one tiny stripe of red along the edge of the cloth because it will be decorated with seeds and embroidery. The married women of the Pow Karen tribe, however, weave designs in coloured wools into their blouses. Across the shoulders a diamond pattern is always used, the only variations being in size, colour and complexity of the diamonds. Below this, another design decorates the front and back of the blouse. This is called the blouse's "wings" and is arranged vertically so that the design looks a little like wings. The intricacy of this weaving usually corresponds to the intricacy of the shoulder patterns, and the women say that the designs get larger and more "ugly" as a woman gets older.[16]

The skirts of the Pwo Karen married women are predominantly red with plain stripes woven in cotton thread, a wide black one down the centre of the cloth and narrower ones of various colours to give variation to the red. Two pieces of cloth are sewn together and used horizontally.

The white dresses of the unmarried Karen girls reach to their ankles but are basically the same style as the shirts. Sometimes these dresses may have a yoke or even — rarely — a waistline, but there is no tailoring involved, simply a joining of straight pieces of cloth, and a marking of the join by a strip of colour. The dresses of the Sgaw Karen girls are very plain with simple edgings of colour, but the dresses of the Pwo Karen girls are often elaborately decorated.

Weaving can be done outdoors because it's only done in the dry season.

Sgaw Karen skirt length from a different region. Natural dye colours vary greatly with the type of plants used.

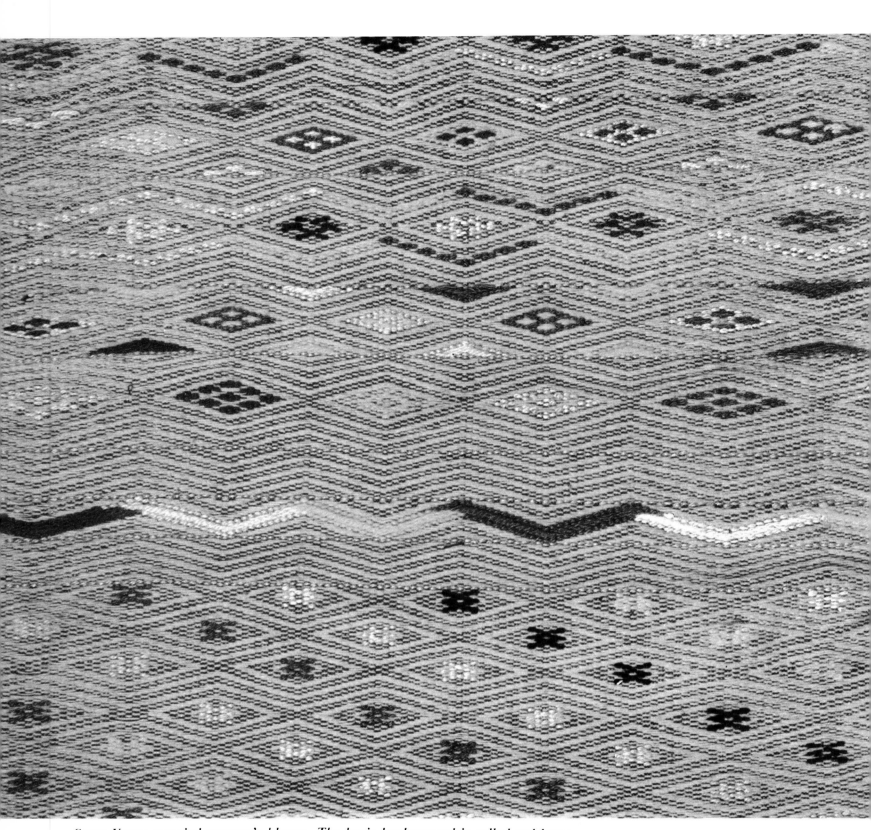

Sgaw Karen married woman's blouse. The basic background is called red leaves.

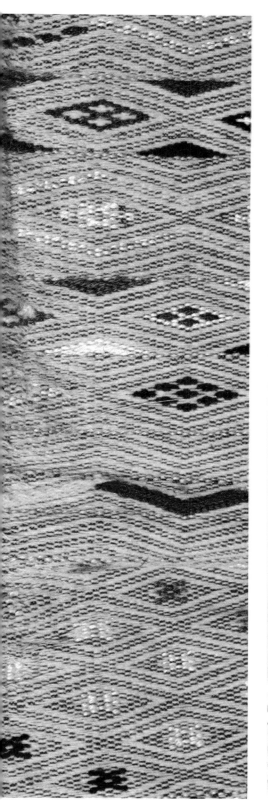

Ginning cotton to remove seeds. The woman is instructing her nieces.

Lawa spinning wheel.

Yao dyeing homespun cloth.

Akha woman preparing the warp for weaving cotton cloth.

Meo woman splitting hemp stalks and joining the strands.

Akha woman spinning cotton into thread as she walks.

Sgaw Karen weaver.

Pwo Karen weaver. Notice tufting on skirt.

Blue Meo woman weaving hemp cloth.

Gue Ba Aka Akha loom.

97

Yer Tung Akha loom.

Ya Khong Akha loom.

Akha winding cotton thread.

Hemp plant cultivated by the Meo for making hemp-fibre cloth.

Akha fish bag (middle right) netted from wild hemp fibre.

"You are as alluring as the fragrance of a pomelo flower," a Pwo Karen song goes. Girl weaving with leather harness.

The khoh *root which is used to produce a brick-red coloured dye.*

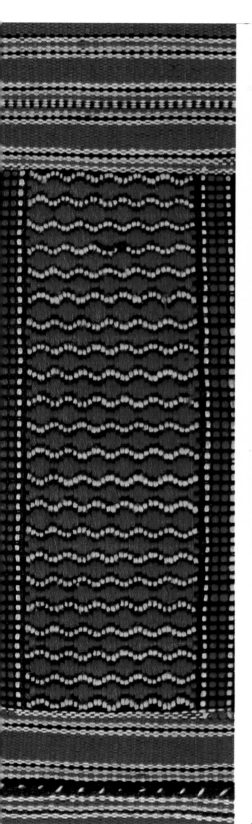

Lawa burial blanket (detail).

Sgaw Karen woven skirt with tin beads.

Red geometrical designs across the shoulders and around the hemlines are made by inserting many tufts of red thread into the cloth as it is being woven and then cutting them off close to form a fluffy raised decoration. From the age of 10, each girl weaves her own dress, and the amount of decoration increases with her age, reaching its most elaborate at the age of courtship. A girl's first dress will have perhaps two narrow red stripes woven above the waist with one strip of diamond-shaped tufted designs in between. By her early twenties there will be three wide stripes with patterns in between as well as many patterns of fluffy tufts. As she gets older the amount of decoration decreases. As one observer has commented: "there is a correlation between age and ornamentation. Decoration is at its height — when beauty is at its height. During childhood and old age it is merely rudimentary, a reflection of undeveloped childhood and the faded beauty of old age."[17] For best effect, a layer of long red tassel is added below the shoulder, hanging to the knee at front and back.

The Karen also weave shoulder bags, in sizes large enough for a man to carry a month's supplies, or small enough to be a lady's purse. A short piece of cloth, perhaps 60 centimetres long, is folded in half, and the two ends of a longer piece are attached to its sides to form the shoulder strap. The bottom of the bag is thus unseamed and able to carry considerable weights. Traditionally these bags were white with red stripes or red with white stripes and no other decoration, and for dress occasions long tassels were left along the bottom and sides. As a result of outside influences, many variations in colour can now be seen, and there are even some woven-in designs appearing.

Women of the Lahu Na and Lahu Shi groups have turned weaving of shoulder bags on the back-strap loom into a major tribal industry. There are two levels of warp threads — one black and one white. Black threads are used for the weft. The resulting cloth is "grey". Any other combination of colours can be used of course — black with a coloured warp, white with a coloured warp, or warp and weft in two different colours. The weaver then forms a pattern by using a small pointed stick to catch and raise certain threads. Perhaps the oldest of these patterns are the six-pointed star, the diamond and the zigzag. An alternative method is to thread both warp and weft with threads of the same colour and add a pattern of a different colour by lifting the threads and inserting a diferent colour of thread only where the pattern is desired. Both types of shoulder bag use cotton thread, but acrylic yarn or wool is preferred for making the pattern, and sometimes embroidery cotton or some other shiny thread is added to give special effects.

The Lahu Nyi prefer to buy material for their clothes, especially when they can find — and can afford — velvet. Whenever possible, they include velvet in their best costumes. Lahu Nyi women use hand-woven striped cloth of fine cotton thread for the top third of their skirts, but this is purchased from the Shans of Burma or from lowland weavers in Chiang Mai or Lamphun provinces. The background of the cloth is red, and multi-colored pinstripes provide a horizontal design. Lahu Shi women also purchase cloth for their costumes.

Women of the Lahu Na group have always been weavers. They have traditionally woven plain or striped homespun cloth using black as the basic colour if the cloth is for a skirt, white or another colour if the cloth is for shirts and blouses. It is only over the last 30 years that they have also made extensive use of the back-strap loom for weaving shoulder bags.

The Yao are the only tribe whose women do not spin, dye or weave. Although they practised these crafts in the past, they have to spend much time embroidering their elaborate pants, and find it easier to buy all their cloth and decorate it with their own distinctive embroidery and applique. For articles to be decorated with cross-stitch embroidery, the Yao usually purchase homespun cloth from other tribeswomen.

Given the difference in types of looms, threads, dyes and methods, it is clear that the term "weaving" is here being stretched to cover a variety of hilltribe skills. At one end of the spectrum is the weaving of simple homespun cloth from unbleached cotton for everyday use; at the other is the making of the Lawa burial blankets with their special dyes, tie-dyed and woven-in patterns and aura of ceremonial secrecy. In between come a wide range of articles made in a wide range of styles. The constant factor used to be that hilltribe women considered weaving to be one of the most basic and necessary of skills. They learned it early and continued to practise it all their lives, perhaps rising to heights of artistry. At the very least they could clothe their families adequately, in itself an impressive achievement. Even today, when a Lawa man dies, his weapons are placed on his grave. When a Lawa woman dies, it is her loom which graces her grave. However, ready-made cloth is now so easily available that weaving is no longer so widely practised. Among the Lahu, Lisu and Yao at least, purchased cloth has become the rule rather than the exception.

At first I thought I could resist you
But your spinning wheel compels me to your side
Like the haunting call of the gibbon.
When the moon climbs above the high mountain,
My feet lead me to your hearth
Before I realise what is happening.
I have fallen in love with you.
If you have any feeling for me,
Bring me three heaps of tobacco
Made from the plant with the silver-tipped leaves.
I will put them in my water pipe
And smoke with pleasure.

White Meo song.

Embroidery

Meo girl learning to embroider.

FAMME'S STOOL is low and the chickens feed so close to her feet that sometimes tiny pieces of their down drift into her basket of threads.

She hunches over her work, needle flashing with the familiar stitches of the border patterns, her mind busy planning the more complex ones to follow. These are no ordinary pants: she is preparing them to wear to the wedding of a distant cousin in a neighbouring village. They are to be the most beautiful in the village: the colours the richest, the patterns the most difficult. Already some of the women have commented on the precision of her stitches and the evenness of the thread.

She puts the finishing touch to the last border pattern and lays the cloth down. Her hand hovers over the threads, hesitating. This is the crucial moment. If Famme is to attract the admiration of that man from her cousin's village her choice now will be all-important.

She thinks back over all the designs and all the colour combinations she has looked at in the last few weeks, trying to choose the most striking. She has asked the best embroiderer in the village for advice, she has visited all the women renowned for their needlework and has stolen surreptitious looks at their work, trying to make a mental picture of the way each one works out her colour scheme. But though this has helped, she still has not made the final decision about her own work. She must choose a combination of colours that will be unusual enough to be remarked upon, but not so different that it makes her the talk of the village.

And most important, her work must make a good impression in his village. Young girls from several villages will be present for the wedding celebration, and Famme knows the competition will be fierce. Though it is the women who gossip about the quality of each newcomer's pants, the men notice, too.

She wonders what colours he really likes best. As a result of many consultations, she has decided to use purple, green and red as the theme of her trousers, but which one should dominate? Her gaze lingers on the purple, for it seems so modern, so dashing. But maybe his mother wouldn't approve, and his sister might judge her to be one of the "fast" set.

She reaches for the red. It is traditional, to be sure, but it is strong, too, and hints at passion and excitement. As the first crosses are stitched onto the dark cloth, she begins to smile confidently. These might turn out to be the finest pants in the world.

Skill with her needle is one of the main ambitions of the Yao girl. Although embroidery is done by women of the Meo, Lahu, Lisu, Karen and Akha tribes, it is never as extensive and seldom as fine as the work of the Yao woman. For her, embroidery has reached the level of an art.

A girl in the Yao tribe learns to embroider at a very early age. When she is four she will be given her first pair of trousers, stitched by her mother with a few simple patterns, and from that time on she may be seen with a needle and a piece of scrap cloth, learning the most important craft of her tribe. By the time she is 10, sitting with idle hands will bring a rebuke from Mother: "You'll have nothing to wear when you grow up!" She begins with the five simplest — and oldest — designs, and only after she has mastered these will she be permitted to attempt the more complex patterns.

Four of these ancient designs are done in weave stitch which appears as a series of parallel lines. The fifth, known as Hunter's Blind, probably developed a little later as a result of experiments in crossing the lines to make a new horizontal cross-stitch. It can be seen as the intermediate step between the simple patterns and the complex diagonal cross-stitch which evolved later and for which the Yao are best known.[18]

At the peak of her ability a Yao woman's greatest pride is the wide variety of cross-stitch designs she has perfected. Well over 100 designs are known. Most of them are used widely, though each village has its favourites. One design, called Tiger Skin, is extremely complicated and denotes great prestige, for only a woman with lots of money can afford the extra thread and the time to do it.

Traditionally the embroidery was done with dyed silk thread on cotton cloth, but mercerised cotton thread or weaving thread with a lustre is now more popular. The traditional colour combination was red, yellow, dark green, dark blue and white. As Yao embroidery relies on colour contrast rather than design contour to form the pattern, a minimum of four or five colours is needed. Today a wide range of colours is used, but never in combinations of more than seven different colours at a time. The Yao also like to use a thread the same colour as their cloth, and the indigo-on-indigo sections of the patterns give a strangely blank effect. A girl's choice of colour combinations is said to reveal her nature, while the quality of her workmanship reveals her to be fastidious or careless, hard-working or lazy, imaginative, docile, quick-tempered. A man is able to find out a great deal about a woman from her embroidery and may even choose his wife by the characteristics portrayed in her pants.

Unlike most of the other hilltribe crafts, Yao embroidery has symbolic as well as a decorative purpose. Every pattern has a name and some recall a legend, and historic occasion, a place of origin or a tribal belief. The explanation for this may well lie in their story of their own past, when they boiled and ate their books as a last resort during a great famine. It may be that embroidery has developed as an alternative to writing as a means of recording the history and traditions of the tribe. If this is so, then every Yao woman is a living history book, for embroidery covers her trousers from waist to mid-calf.

Apart from the five basic patterns which usually

Detail of weaving-style embroidery on Meo funeral costume (sleeve).

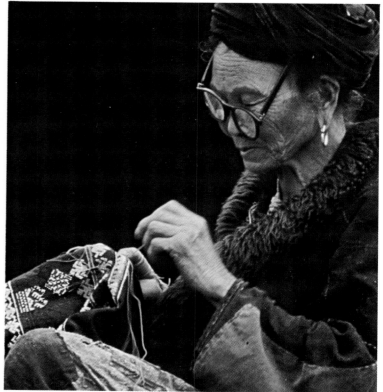

Yao woman stitching a new pair of trousers.

appear at the edge of the trouser embroidery, any combination of patterns (and colours!) seems to be acceptable. Although some designs are peculiar to certain areas, and women from other areas cannot do them, the women say they choose "whatever looks pretty". It is interesting to speculate whether combinations of patterns were once more rigidly prescribed or whether the women have always been so free to choose the designs — and hence the version of history, perhaps — that appealed to them. All embroidery is done from the wrong side of the cloth, and though they are experts with their own patterns, this results in some curious "mirror image" effects if they try to embroider a name or copy a picture from a book. The women do not use scissors, breaking the threads with their teeth, and because the work has no knots, the design looks complete viewed from the back as well as the front.

Children's hats are also extensively embroidered. By the time she is old enough to have children, a woman is likely to be an expert with her needle. Though her children may wear nothing else they will each have a hat as colourful as she can make it.

Embroidery also appears on horse cruppers, on the last 45 centimetres or so of women's turbans and on sashes — usually widely spaced "floweret" style patterns. Small patterns also appear on New Year aprons. Each man has one complete pattern worked on the lower right front corner of his jacket.

The Meo use about a dozen complex cross-stitch designs, most of them similar to the Yao designs. They can be told apart because Yao stitching is always of uniform size, as it is always done on homespun. Meo stitching may be larger or smaller because it is done on many kinds of materials. A design which the Yao call Meo Forks is very popular with both tribes.

Blue Meo women embroider the lower edge of their batik skirts, the collars of their jackets, the tops of their baby carriers, and stitch the closing edge of the man's jacket with particularly rich and brilliant patterns. The men also like to have the ends of their sashes decorated, and the wide ends are usually covered with solid embroidery, folded on a bias so as to come to a point, and allowed to hang in a triangular shape in front of their trousers. On festive occasions these sashes blossom with gay designs rivalled only by the brightly embroidered "bibs" of the women.

White Meo embroidery is usually extremely small and fine. The women use it on their own turbans, on the hats of their children, and on the ends of the sashes of both men and women. The Meo often use embroidery as a complement to their applique work, to set off the applique patterns and to make the work look fuller. The whole is then "framed" by bands of coloured cloth.

Karen embroidery appears only on the seeded blouses of the married women (see Chapter 9).

The Lisu embroider the courting bags carried by young men, the padded cloth triangles from which the tassels on a woman's turban hang, and the small bags used by

Even in the same village, styles vary. These men's sashes were all photographed in one Meo village in a single morning.

Men's sash.

Yao women's trousers.

Yao woman working near her house.

Detail of a Yao sacred scroll painting with Yao embroidery
designs.

Yao bridal veil.

Yao embroidery sampler with composite designs.

White Meo embroidery.

*Ya Khong Akha
embroidery on jackets.*

*The five basic designs for the border
of Yao women's trousers.*

Embroidery on Karen blouse.

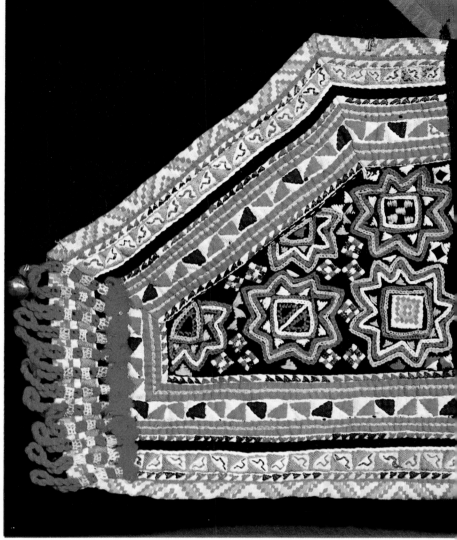

Detail of front piece of a Meo men's jacket.

Embroidery on a Lisu women's bag for carrying silver coins.

115

116

Detail of Yao women's trouser panel.

Sometimes one pair of spectacles isn't enough.

women for carrying silver coins. Lisu stitches are usually tiny zig-zags, so meticulously executed that they look machine-made, and depend on colour combinations for effect.

Lahu embroidery also relies on colour rather than design for its impact. Though Lahu Na women occasionally use some cross-stitch, it is only used to form simple lines of Xs. Satin stitch forms the scalloped edges of the applique work on Lahu Na shoulder bags. Chain, running and single line stitches are more common. Women of the Lahu Nyi group use many rows of these stitches, alternating colours and stitching to decorate the deep borders of their skirts.

Embroidery is found even on Yao horse crupper.

Applique decorations are the most striking feature on the clothes of Lahu Na women, but they do embroider floral or geometric designs in a wide border on the lower edges of their tunics. They work similar designs, or sometimes star shapes, predominantly red, on the lower edges of both trousers and jackets of their men.

Women of the Lahu Shehleh group use chain stitch to embroider the cream-coloured borders of their tunics and trousers, and also embroider a five-centimetre strip along only the back hem of their long tunics. Women of the Lahu Shi group use chain stitch and flowerets to embroider the front and lower edges of their short black jackets and embroider a small circle at the top of the set-in flare over each hip. A tiny silver half-sphere stud is sewn in the centre of each circle.

The Akha embroider the jackets and shoulder bags of both men and women, and the women's leggings. One group of Akha, the Ya Khong from Pa Mee village, embroider geometrical designs on narrow strips of cloth and then sew the strips in rows onto the backs of their jackets. The designs appear intricate but depend more on the use of many tiny stitches and great variety in colour than on complex embroidery stitches. Chain, running and zig-zag stitches are the most common. Other Akha groups, the Yer Tung and Gue Ba embroider straight onto the cloth of the jackets, creating a striped effect by alternating rows of applique and silver half-sphere studs with lines of simple embroidery. All the Akha groups prefer to use strong basic colours, especially red, blue and green, in their embroidery.

By skilful use of colour contrasts and very fine stitches, hilltribe embroiderers can produce spectacular results. However, they have never explored beyond the possibilities of their three or four basic stitches. There seems to be no use of knotting or looping techniques and none of the more complicated stitchery found in other cultures.

My dear beautiful sister, why are you still
bending to embroider your dark cloth?
Don't you hear the bells of the horses which carry me here?
Listen! My horse neighs and rears when he sees a mare
in your stable.
I am a stranger from a faraway village;
I am very tired.
I have come to see your face, your smile when you greet
your guests.
Your face is like the purple poppy flower
Unfolding a greeting to the morning sun.
Please bring me a stool to sit on, and pour me some green tea.
If the golden leaf of the tobacco is ready, please
bring it to me.
I will smoke the water pipe and enjoy its sweet flavour
before I go.

Yao song

Yer Tung Akha jacket is richly appliqued.

THE SHAMAN was at his wits' end. He had sacrificed a pig and several chickens to appease the spirits. He had killed a goat to invoke the protection of a special guardian spirit. He had suspended wooden battle swords, spirit-sized, over the main door, and put the head of a dog on a bamboo pole beside the house so that its stench was everywhere. But nothing was working to keep away the jungle demons who sought Lao-ger's soul. At last the patient's license to live expired and there was nothing for it but to begin preparations for the funeral.

Lao-ger's wife, Muey, was too busy to mourn. She sent word to all members of his clan, even those in the most distant Meo villages. She arranged for someone to show his soul the road to the afterworld. Her neighbours arrived to help, and her eldest son supervised the allocation of tasks to them, for some duties had to be performed by people of different clans. Everyone set to with a will, cooking food and making offerings to the spirits.

The body had to be washed, and all the gold teeth extracted so that they would not cause a birthmark in the next reincarnation. Muey sat the body on a bench and her son pulled the teeth with tongs borrowed from the silversmith.

Then it was time to dress Lao-ger in his funeral jackets. Muey had started making them years before, but the hemp cloth was still shiny and new for of course they had never been worn. The first jacket had long sleeves, the second had elbow-length sleeves, the third was sleeveless. Once they were all in place they looked like a single garment. Lao-ger looked so splendid in the bright colours, so dignified in death. Muey looked tenderly at him. She was glad now that she had spent so many months making the applique design especially intricate. She was proud that her husband would go so finely dressed.

Lao-ger was placed on a waist-high bamboo platform against the side wall of the house. His eldest son put his favourite flintlock gun beside the body, and his daughter laid his neckrings on his chest. Food and drink were set at his head.

Now the mourners gathered and the laments began. Lao-ger's virtues were recited at length, his praises sung, his departure mourned. A drum beat a solemn accompaniment throughout. Muey was gratified, for the noise was tremendous, the praise lavish. Best of all, each of her three sons sacrificed an ox, each tying his animal to his father's body with a piece of white string. This made it a most distinguished and memorable funeral. It also meant Muey would be able to give a big piece of meat to those who had spent long hours chanting truly impressive lamentations, and to those who had helped shoo flies away from the body. She felt very content.

After five days of ceremonies and feasts, it was time for Lao-ger to travel to his burial site, a perfect spot with a view of two mountain tops in perfect alignment. Lao-ger would rest easily there. While some of the men fired guns to salute his soul, others lifted the body and formed a procession. A musician led the way, playing a mournful song on his pan pipes. Lao-ger's niece followed carrying a burning brand. About halfway to the burial site, she turned and ran back, dropping the brand across the path so that the soul could not return to the village. Now Lao-ger was finally gone.

Muey felt lost. The bustle of the funeral was over and there was nothing more for her to do. Now she had time to grieve, too much time. She could not even turn to her needlework for consolation. During the twelve-day mourning period she knew a working needle would prick the body of her husband, and its thread would entangle his legs and hamper him in his journey to the next world. There was nothing to do but sit silently and mourn. Or perhaps she let her mind reach for the thought — perhaps she should begin planning another sumptuous funeral costume . . . her own.

One of the most vivid handicrafts of the hills is applique, the intricate two and three-dimensional work of the Meo, Lahu Na and Yer Tung Akha. It consists of shapes cut from one material and stitched onto another. The patterns, in contrasting colours, are often several layers deep. The Yao make occasional use of this form of decoration.

Other Lahu and Akha groups, and the Lisu people, use a related technique, stitching narrow strips of cloth to form borders and stripes. The appearance of this work is quite different from applique and will therefore be treated as a separate technique and referred to as "banding"

The Meo use applique to decorate the clothes of men, women and children. It is always done with bold colours so that the effect is striking and three-dimensional. Red predominates, and is often placed between black and white so

Lahu Shehleh women'a tunic: bottom edge.

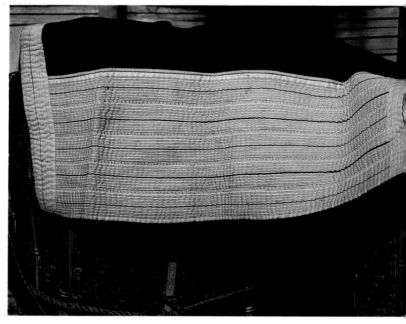

that it looks especially vivid. Gold, shocking pink and either green or blue are other frequently-used colours. The simplest form of applique is seen on the batik skirts of the Blue Meo women, where small geometrical shapes are cut from red or shocking pink cloth and stitched so that they cover parts of the batik pattern. Small diamonds of applique are also included in the embroidered border around the bottom of this skirt.

Much more elaborate applique is prepared for the jackets of both men and women of this group. Each piece is made like a picture, complete in itself, and then stitched to the garment. The base piece is a large rectangle or triangle of cloth, often cut into a zigzag along one side. Strips of various colours are added around the edge of the base piece and small cut-out pieces are added in layers in the centre forming geometrical patterns. These appliqued pieces are used to edge the front openings of the jacket, and the

Yer Tung Akha jacket.

women also sew one, usually square shaped, at the back of the neck of their jackets, sailor style. Tradition dictates that this piece of applique be worn face down on the garment. If there was once a reason for this, it is now forgotten and the women say they do it only to keep it clean, though they can offer no explanation for why they do not show similar concern for the pieces at the front. Some say that only a woman's husband may lift this reversed collar, but others just laugh at such a quaint idea and unhesitatingly lift their collars to show off their handiwork. On the burial costume, this collar is never reversed.

An unusual addition to the applique work of the Blue Meo women is the fragile fabric obtained by unrolling the cocoon of the silkworm. Meo groups usually obtain these cocoons from Northeastern Thai silk growers. A tablet of chemical dye, usually yellow but occasionally bright pink, is dissolved in boiling water and the cocoon is dipped into this, then dried in the sun. The small, soft pieces of tissue-like cloth are then incorporated into the applique. This use of cocoon gives added textural dimension to the work.

Embroidery is also used on the applique, sometimes as an additional ornament on some of the small pieces, sometimes to fill or give emphasis to an area that appears too naked. There seem to be no rules governing the use of either the designs or the materials used in the applique, and a woman can combine them in any way that appeals to her sense of beauty. Cloth printed with small geometrical shapes to resemble Meo applique has recently appeared on the market in Thailand and some Meo women are buying it. The appearance of this "convenience" is a potential threat to the continued existence of Meo applique.

The Blue Meo applique the women's aprons, children's hats and baby carriers. It is interesting to note that the Meo take more time than any other tribe to make special articles for their babies. They also "diaper" the baby by wrapping it in a cloth before binding it onto its mother's back. Perhaps a desire to protect the meticulous workmanship of their batik-and-applique carriers gives these women an interest in infant hygiene that is not shared by women of some other tribes who carry their babies in any old skirt length.

Although technically they belong to the same tribe, the women of the White Meo group have a very different style of applique. They prefer curving spiral shapes, cut from a layer of fine, thin cloth to expose cloth of a different colour underneath. The patterns on White Meo applique are usually much smaller and finer than the Blue Meo equivalents, and as might be expected, the dominant colour is white. Like the Blue Meo, they put applique mainly on their jackets, and wear a larger and more elaborate version of the reversed "sailor" collar.

The Lahu Na use both types of pieced work. The women prepare their applique in pieces five centimeters wide and a metre or more long. Each piece is marked into many small squares, and within each square tiny geometri-

White Meo unmarried girl's cap with "snail shell" applique.

Yao baby carriers adapted for use as glamorous shoulder wraps for festival.

Detail of Lahu Na applique.

Lahu Shehleh banding on sleeve.

Lahu Sheleh leggings.

Blue Meo funeral costume.

125

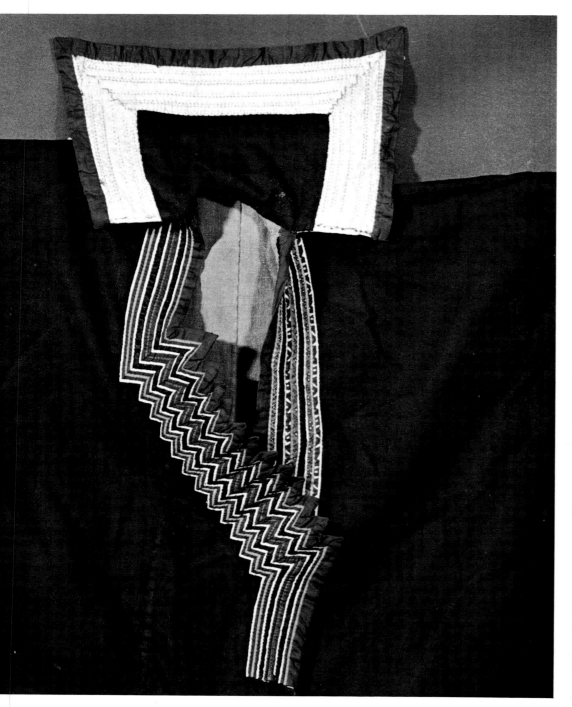

Blue Meo blouse. Note reversed collar.

Blue Meo baby carrier.

Lisu woman's tunic yoke.

Detail of White Meo woman's sash.

White Meo snail pattern applique.

127

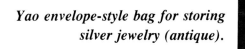

Yao envelope-style bag for storing silver jewelry (antique).

128

Detail of Meo applique with yellow cocoon fabric .

White Meo applique design called bouw chua *(reverie).*

White Meo blouse collar.

129

cal shapes are stitched in layers. These long applique pieces are used as multi-coloured borders down the front opening edges of their black tunics. The dominant colour is usually red, with a plentiful use of white and black for contrast, and dashes of blue, gold or green according to a woman's whim. Bands of cloth in various colours form the lower half of the sleeves, and also appear as stripes or zigzags on the skirts worn under these tunics. Lahu Na shoulder bags are traditionally made of black cloth with applique sewn across the front and back of the bag to give a striped effect. The shoulder strap is made from striped material woven on a back-strap loom.

Akha women of the Yer Tung group decorate the backs of the jackets of both men and women with row after row of applique sewn in diamond and triangle shapes, each piece sewn with minute plain stitches, the colour of the thread contrasting in each row with the colour of the cut-out so that the stitching becomes part of the overall design. (The other applique experts — the Meo and Black Lahu — take great care to hide their stitches!) Lines of embroidery are sometimes interspersed among the rows of applique. The layers of cloth give a quilted or padded effect to the jackets. The appliqued area is outlined with a border of greyish-white Job's Tears seeds, and may be further decorated with seashells, white buttons, and silver half-sphere studs sewn in triangle patterns. The sleeves of the women's jackets are usually banded with strips of cloth in several colours, while the only colour on the men's arms is the red or blue binding of the cuffs.

Banding is the only kind of applique done by the other Akha groups. Strips of cloth of various colours and widths form stripes on the sleeves, shoulders and lower edges of the jackets, and similar pieces decorate the leggings of the women. The rough edges of the jackets, leggings and sashes are bound with strips of cloth which thus serve a practical as well as a decorative purpose. Although the colours are bright, and variety is added by interspersing rows of embroidery, buttons, and even dyed feathers, the bands of cloth are usually wide — maybe as much as five centimetres — and widely spaced, and the work lacks the intricacy and delicacy that characterises the applique of the Yer Tung Akha.

The Lahu Shehleh also do banding. They edge the women's long black tunics with a five centimetre band made from white and pale yellow cloth, sometimes highlighted with a very narrow strip of red or green. Bands of pale yellow cloth are also used around the wrist and upper arm, across the shoulder line and waistline, and bind the lower edges of their leggings. This use of pale colours is in marked contrast to the bright colour schemes of most other groups, and adds a touch of distinction. The effect is achieved by fine stitching and by colour, rather than by intricacy of design.

Women of the Lahu Shi group also use bands of cloth to decorate their costumes. The wide black centrepiece of their skirts is often adorned with white zigzags or brightly-coloured flower shapes. Strips of bright cloth are used to form stripes on the sleeves and around the body of the black jackets.

Lahu Nyi do a line of embroidery spanning two bands of colour for added effect.

The most extensive use of banding, however, is seen on the tunics of the Lisu women. Using fabric of many different colours, they sew narrow strips together to a width of as much as 30 centimetres, creating an impressive rainbow of cloth. Instead of then being superimposed on the finished tunic in a purely decorative role, this multi-coloured piece is incorporated into the body of the garment, forming the upper sleeves and yoke. The "skirt" of the tunic is made from plain cloth, either blue or green, and these colours, together with black, white, red and yellow, predominate in the banded yoke. The lower sleeves and the leggings of this costume are always red, and bands of cloth form the borders on the lower edges of the red cloth. Caps for small children are also made from narrow strips sewn together, and bands of colour edge the leggings worn by the men at New Year, but this form of decoration is primarily a feature of the women's clothes. In recent years Lisu banding had become increasingly elaborate, girls vying with each other to see who can fit the most rows of cloth on the yoke. Their attempts at improvisation continue to be limited by the traditional requirement that the basic colour of the yoke be black, and any girls who try to vary *that* are quickly ordered into line by their mothers.

Yao applique is used on the elaborate apron which is worn by the women at weddings and at New Year. It is a decorative rather than practical piece and may be worn in front as an apron or in back as a back cover or baby carrier. These aprons are made of navy blue cotton and decorated with shapes cut from red cloth and elaborately embellished with white silk braid. The bold colours and ornate shapes combine to make this applique work very striking, though it is essentially simple work, using only one layer of cloth for each design and demanding little finesse with the needle because of the relatively large size of each piece. Whereas a Lahu Na woman may be working with pieces of cloth one centimetre square, the Yao woman works with a piece ten centimetres square. Embroidery, tassels and silver half-sphere studs are interspersed with the appliqued shapes to create a highly decorated apron reserved for use on festive occasions. The only other banding on Yao costumes is on the sleeves and lower edges of the men's jackets and the women's tunics.

In all hilltribe applique, colour is of prime interest, from the careful piecework of the Meo to the painstaking work with tiny coloured strips of the Lisu, and all the variations in between. The Meo have introduced a new texture by adding silk cocoon, and several groups mix applique with other types of decoration, but the impact of the applique depends above all on colour contrast.

Batik and Ikat

THERE WAS A stir in the village and Mai looked up from her work. A tourist had appeared, out of nowhere it seemed. Mai sighed. The village had so many visitors these days it was hardly a novelty any more. She lowered her head again and concentrated on putting the finishing touches to her new skirt.

It was a beauty: heavy, richly dyed, brilliantly decorated with applique. She ran her hand over it with pride. Some of the women in her village were taking short-cuts these days, making skirts from light cotton cloth or even – imagine! – buying cloth with batik designs printed on it. They usually sold those skirts to tourists, for they were too proud to wear such shoddy things themselves. Mai envied them the money but was outraged that they should demean the Meo heritage by making imitations. She knew she would never stoop to such things.

As her needle worked at the embroidered border she thought back to the day, nearly two years ago, when she had begun making this skirt. It had been a hot April morning when she planted the hemp seeds, dreaming of the gorgeous skirt they would someday become. The plants had taken three months to grow to the right height and it had taken weeks of work to prepare a soft thread from the tough stalks. Then more weeks waxing on the designs for the batik, a whole month for repeated dyeings, and hours and hours to add the mosaic of applique.

The skirt embodied the rhythm of nature for her. She had worked on it devotedly during the rainy season, but during planting and harvesting had only been able to snatch odd moments for it. The skirt had its seasons, just like everything else in her life.

But now it was nearly complete. For the last four months she had bent over the embroidery, the crowning touch, and within a few days it would be finished. What a prized piece it was!

She paused and leaned back against the wall of her house, letting her work lie across her knees as she watched the young tourist with his following of curious children. He was making his way from house to house, looking at the women's handiwork, nodding and gesturing in the odd mute way of foreigners who couldn't speak the Meo tongue. Soon he was standing before Mai, admiring her skirt. She held it out, pleased to show off the neat pleats and superb colours, conscious of her superior workmanship. The stranger burbled at her in his strange language, nodding and stroking the skirt with his hand, clearly impressed. Mai was gratified.

With a smooth gesture the young man pulled four notes from his pocket and offered them to her. He wanted to buy her skirt! Mai stared at the money. She needed it very badly and it was tempting. Then she lifted her head and stared comtemptuously at the stranger. This was the same amount given for the imitation skirts. He could not even tell the difference.

With all the dignity of her tribe in the movement, she gathered herself up and turned away, stirring indignant curls of dust with her heels as she vanished inside her house.

Batik is a complex craft practised only by the women of the Blue Meo group, and even among them only two or three women in any village are skilled at the art. Adeptness at batik guarantees a high bride price, and increases a woman's status among women and her attractiveness to men.

The process of making batik begins with the preparation of suitable cloth. Although cotton is the most readily available cloth in the hills, Meo women prefer cloth woven from hemp fibres (see Chapter 5) because of its weight and glossiness. The batiked cloth is used almost exclusively for the heavily pleated skirts of the women, so it is prepared in pieces six metres long and 30 centimetres wide.

The surface of the cloth is divided into squares with a pointed marker. It may be a piece of metal or bamboo, but the favourite tool is a one-Baht aluminium spoon pur-

Blue Meo baby carrier.

chased from a lowland market. Wax designs are applied within these squares. The wax is harvested from jungle beehives, and applied with a special instrument made from a single piece of bent copper attached to a bamboo handle. Although it appears to be a simple device, a great deal of skill is involved in making it, for the wax pen must permit an even and free flow of wax. Not even as many as one man per village is able to make these pens.

The wax is applied in short straight strokes, so that it flows evenly and in just the right thickness. After several strokes the pen must be dipped again into the pot of warm wax. No curves are ever drawn on Meo batik, and the only element other than straight lines is a dot, which is sometimes drawn in clusters around other parts of the pattern. The women who draw the patterns must have a sure eye and a steady hand, for there are no aids such as rulers available to make their work easier.

Although the women create an almost infinite number of patterns when they batik, all of the patterns arise from

The waxing finished, this cloth is now ready to be dyed indigo. The differences in colour are due to different batches of tinted wax.

seven basic designs which are combined in different ways according to a woman's imagination. The original meanings of the designs have been lost, at least among the Meo in Thailand. Only their names are still remembered — Python, Pumpkin Flower, Sun Ray, Star, Fern, Silver Flower and Seashell — and are faithfully passed down through the generations.

Once the wax has been applied, the material can be dyed. After it has been boiled to remove the wax, the dark cloth has delicate white designs. The indigo-coloured wax is saved and used to tint the next batch of wax for batiking.

To add further colour, the Meo women usually cover certain parts of the batik design with fine red applique. About 12 centimetres of white material is added to one side of the batik and 12 centimetres of embroidered cloth to the other, in order to make it wide enough for a skirt.

The skirt length is then pleated by being dipped in rice starch, and pressed with flat stones. The pleats are basted first, then folded accordion-style. When the basting threads are pulled tight, the skirt is compacted for easy storage.

These batik skirts are one of the signs of wealth in a Meo household. It requires about two hours' concentrated effort just to wax one 15 centimetre square of cloth, so that it can take from six months to a year to complete a skirt. Possession of more than one of these skirts is an affirmation of affluence, and even the wealthiest of women is unlikely to have more than five.

Before a Meo bride leaves her parents' home on her wedding day, she displays all the possessions she is going to take with her to her husband's home. Her pleated skirts are a featured part of this display.

The only other use to which this highly prized batik is put is as the centrepiece of the baby carrier, where a square of batiked cloth is edged with bands of bright cloth to a size of approximately 37 by 35 centimetres. The surface of the batik may be left plain or may be decorated with gay pom-poms or tiny applique designs. A smaller rectangle, about 25 by 17 centimetres, with a centrepiece of embroidery, is attached to the top of the carrier and long ties are stitched to either side of this so that the mother can tie her baby securely to her back.

A related craft is the process of ikat or tie-dye, which is practised by just two tribes, the Karen and the Lawa. They do not tie-dye entire lengths of cloth, but rather the threads they use for weaving certain garments.

Sgaw Karen use a natural dye in the tie-dyeing of thread for the married woman's skirt. This craft has long been associated with spirit worship and it is very difficult for outsiders to gather any information about it. The women refuse to discuss it for fear of having their dyes spoiled by offended spirits. As a result, it has remained one of the best-kept secrets of the hills. The following details

Marking on the wax designs with a special pen.

The dyed, batiked cloth hanging up to dry.

Akha woman dyeing homespun cloth.

Lawa skirt length with woven pattern formed by indigo tie-dyed thread.

Blue Meo baby carrier in use.

Sgaw Karen woman preparing threads for ikat (tie-dyeing).

have been gleaned from Karens who have converted to Christianity.

The popular brick red dye is prepared from crushed root of the *kho* plant. Women are careful not to touch oil the day before, or to speak during the dyeing process, believing this might cause the colour to be uneven. This is probably also an exercise in concentration. Bamboo stalks are cut into the shape of a "hand" with extended fingers, and the threads are wound between the corresponding fingers of each "hand". Then the threads are pulled from one finger at a time and tied together, and the whole skein is then dipped into the boiling dye. A woman works alone at tie-dyeing, usually away from the village, seeing and speaking to no one, and the thread she dyes is only for her own skirt. The pattern woven from these threads is called Crab or Python Skin. So time-consuming is the tie-dye process that the present trend is toward weaving the "four-finger-width" stripes with plain red thread, reserving the tie-dyed threads for the one-centimetre stripes in between. The reverse was the fashion a generation ago: wide tie-dyed stripes separated by one-centimetre red stripes.

The Sgaw Karen loop their undyed threads around a bamboo pole, then tie the threads at regular intervals with fibres from a leaf called *ton-nor-e,* which must be boiled first to give it the requisite strength.

The Lawa tribe uses tie-dyed thread in the burial

Pleating on a completed Meo skirt.

blankets that shroud a dead body while it lies in state — three to seven days. The secret of the dyes and designs used for these blankets remains the exclusive property of one family, and no one in the village would try to learn the secrets for fear of the bad omens associated with death.

The natural dyes used for these burial blankets produce soft muted colours — pinkish brown, pale corn yellow, pink, blue and grey. These threads are used to weave one-centimetre stripes close to the edges of the blankets.

Lawa weavers make women's skirts from homespun cotton, and incorporate some tie-dye patterns in them. The cloth is basically indigo or black, with tie-dyed bands of blue and white. The popular patterns are called lightning designs, and may be woven in red instead of blue.

The deep blue-black dye that most of the tribes use to colour their homespun cloth comes from the indigo plant (Indigofera tinctoria). It sprouts about the time of the first rains, late in April. There are two crops, one harvested in June and the other in late October. There are two strains of indigo plant, the native one and what the tribespeople refer to as the 'communist' type, because it was originally imported from Vietnam. Both strains produce a good dye.

When ready for harvesting, the indigo bush stands about 60 centimetres high. The branches are cut and put to soak in water in a wooden barrel for three or four days. After the second night the branches must be turned over so that they soak evenly. Then the whole is poured into lime, which absorbs the colour of the plant and acts as the medium for the dye. The water and branches are then discarded. During the liming period there is a very strong smell from the decaying branches.

Then an alkaline water is prepared. Ashes are mixed with water and stirred well. When the ashes settle, the water is poured off and is ready for use. This water is mixed with the lime, which is now blue and liquid. One glass of rice whiskey is added to the mixture and it is left to sit for two or three days.

The whiskey used for this purpose must be strong: more than 35 degrees of alcohol (70 proof). After two or three days, fermentation bubbles will appear. If the bubbles are strong and do not break easily, the dye is ready to use. If the bubbles are weak, more rice whiskey must be added.

When the dye is ready to use, the material is soaked in water and dipped into the indigo mixture for about half an hour, then removed and allowed to dry in the wind, away from direct sunlight. This dip and dry, dip and dry process is repeated on an average of two to four times per day, depending on the weather.

After about 30 dippings and dryings, the cloth has absorbed enough dye. It is then washed twice in clear water and is ready to use. Usually indigo-dyed cloth runs for the first two or three washings and after that the colour is set forever.

Flower design on Karen married woman's seeded blouse.

NORDEYNYA was as beautiful as the wild lily for which she had been named. She knew that the young school teacher, Kru Manit, thought so. Ever since he had come up from the lowlands to teach in the Karen Village, she had been conscious of his admiration. He was always watching when she came back from fishing, her blouse wet against her body, and he always had a special word of thanks for her gifts of vegetables, even when his kitchen was overflowing with similar presents from other villagers.

And now his proposal was being presented to her father. The headman had agreed to act as emissary. Although Kru Manit was an outsider and therefore forbidden to marry into the tribe, everyone liked him and was prepared to risk the calamities that such a marriage might bring to the village. To get around the problem, the headman had proclaimed that Kru Manit was now his "son" and had come in person to negotiate a betrothal. Nordeynya pressed her ear to the wall, the better to eavesdrop.

"Is there anything the matter? Your visit comes as a surprise," said her father, opening the ritual conversation in the traditional way.

The headman sighed. "Oh, we hear you have some good, sweet fruit trees. We would like to have a cutting for propagation."

"Yes, we have some fruit trees, but I am not sure how good they are. They might be rotten, not worth having."

"We don't mind, as long as we can have a cutting from your tree."

"How can I refuse if you keep insisting?" shrugged her father. And the pact was sealed.

Nordeynya was pleased and excited. She had already prepared wedding clothes for herself and her groom, and soon now they would be brought out of the storage basket. She ignored the small shiver of foreboding that came with the thought. Surely nothing could mar the match. Outsider or not, he was her ideal husband: clever, handsome, popular.

Once her parents had tied a white thread and a silver bell around the wrists of Kru Manit and his best man, the whole village knew for sure what they had guessed for months – there was to be a wedding. They opened the first bottles of rice wine at once and began the first of several bouts of heavy drinking which would culminate at the wedding feast.

When the wedding day arrived, everyone turned out to take part, Kru Manit's friends dressed up in their best clothes and formed a noisy parade, singing, dancing, playing horns, drums and gongs, slowly heading for Nordeynya's house. Kru Manit walked in their midst wearing his oldest clothes, a humble beggar in appearance, a proud victor in his thoughts. He had overcome so many fears and taboos to arrive at this moment, he had won the battle for trust and friendship and love – his step was jubilant.

Suddenly, a huge black snake slid across the path. The procession stopped abruptly and everyone stared in silence, horrified at the bad omen, pale with apprehension. But the headman stepped forward bravely and spoke to the snake: "You go your way and we'll go ours. Your way is short and evil, ours is long and pleasant." And he spat on the path. The tension broke and gradually the noise level rose again. Kru Manit tried not to notice the worried glances, the muffled whispers around him. He fixed his thoughts on Nordeynya and strode on.

As they approached the bride's house, her mother came to sprinkle water on their feet as a reminder of the coolness and pleasantness of life. She had placed a stone inside the bowl of water to bring the added gift of longevity. Then she welcomed them to her home, and they settled themselves in pairs, a friend of the bride beside a friend of the groom.

Nordeynya came shyly forward with a lacquered bamboo bowl of water. She washed Kru Manit's hands, then brought a dish of chicken and rice and spooned him a mouthful. As soon as he accepted it, the hush was broken by cheers and laughter and everyone began to eat and drink. Soon the party was in full swing, all thoughts of trouble for-

Sgaw Karen married woman stitches seeds onto a new blouse.

gotten. At the height of the merriment, someone fetched a bucket of water and unceremoniously dumped it all over Kru Manit. The sight of the dripping bridegroom was the signal for his wedding clothes to be brought out – the red woven shirt, the turban and trousers that Nordeynya had prepared for him. He was transformed into a proud husband, and the merrymakers surrounded him, louder and happier than ever.

On the second day, Kru Manit opened the ceremonies by pouring wine for Nordeynya, and once she had sipped it shyly, everyone began drinking in earnest. The headman presented them with a pair of curved silver bars as a token of the prosperity they would enjoy together, and this called for another round of drinks. Before long, Kru Manit was so drunk that the only thing he could remember was the blessing he had received from all the elders in turn: "May you have ten sons and a thousand grandchildren." He was too dizzy to know how to respond to that, let alone to join the exuberant dancers who had climbed onto the roof of the house to continue their celebrations.

Necklace of long Job's Tears mixed with fried reed.

But his mind cleared rapidly when Nordeynya appeared in her marriage clothes. She had put on the red striped skirt and the black blouse, heavy with seed embroidery, that proclaimed her a married woman at last. Kru Manit could not take his eyes off her loveliness. How had he been so lucky as to defy the old laws and win this girl? How had she been so courageous as to accept him? They must surely have a special destiny, he thought proudly.

And they had. With an ominous creak, the flimsy bamboo house collapsed. It was a truly memorable party.

A shiny white seed that grows in the jungle is prized by Karen women, who use it to decorate the jackets they don after marriage. These seeds, known in English as Job's Tears, come in various shapes — round, long, oval — and sizes ranging from very tiny to as much as one centimetre in length and half a centimetre in diameter. The seeds can also be greyish-white or brownish-grey in colour. In some places, these seeds are also a cultivated crop. The plants stand about two metres tall at maturity.

The part used by the Karens is actually the outer shell of the seed, and when the kernel is pulled out, the small hole that is left is just big enough for a needle to pass through. The Karen believe that if they harvest Job's Tears during the waning of the moon, the hole in the seed will be larger and the sewing job easier.

The meticulous craftswoman first dries the seeds in the embers of the fire for about two weeks to get them perfectly white. Less careful workers omit this process. The seeds are then sorted into groups according to size and shape. Each seed must be examined for cracks, a tedious task.

The round seeds are the most practical because they don't crack, and are very popular for stringing necklaces. They come in two sizes and children like to eat the larger ones which are edible when they are young. The long ones are preferred for use on jackets because they offer more interesting design potential. When the sorting process is complete, the women begin sewing the long seeds onto their dark blouses in a variety of patterns.

The pattern names are purely descriptive of the design — Zigzag, Set at Diagonals, Closely-sewn Seeds, Standing Horizontal. Only the pattern known as Dog's Footprint offers a more picturesque name. The lines marking the width of each pattern are usually stitched first, and then the seeded patterns are positioned. The bottom of the blouse will usually be edged with two or three very narrow rows of seed work, often done in zigzag pattern.

The seedwork is always accompanied by embroidery which is used to fill the spaces between the seeded patterns. There are perhaps half a dozen traditional embroidered patterns worked in satin stitch, whose names are also purely functional: making a circle, making a rectangle, making triangles, making a four-cornered pattern. More

Blouses of Sgaw Karen married women. The designs vary from village to village.

144

An old seeded blouse wrapped around the base of a papaya tree to encourage it to bear fruit.

evocative names such as pumpkin flower, armadillo and snowflake have been given to these embroidered patterns by outsiders for ease of identification, but for the tribespeople themselves there is no special meaning or symbolism in any of their patterns and no deliberate attempt to reproduce designs from the natural world.

Natural dyes are available only in five or six colours, plus undyed white, and traditionally these colours have dominated the embroidery on seeded jackets. Chemical dyes, however, have gradually been making their appearance, adding brilliant pinks, lemon yellow, green and blue. Karen women seem particularly fond of bright blue, perhaps because it was unknown to them until fairly recently.

A few generations ago, Job's Tears were an important status symbol, reserved for older women, but today any married woman may wear them. Yet in spite of the beauty of the seeded blouse and the new status it gives a woman, a bride always makes a great show of reluctance over putting it on for the first time. She will loudly proclaim the beauty

Detail from Akha woman's headdress showing three shapes of Job's Tears and two types of red seed.

of her white dress, and only after much hesitation and coaxing from her friends will she agree to change for her wedding ceremony, even though she has spent weeks making her first blouse as intricately decorated and brilliantly coloured as possible.

The Meo bride makes a similar show of reluctance prior to her wedding. She will disclaim any interest in the man she is to marry, and finally has to be dragged to her new home by the bridegroom's elders. Sometimes she may even hide from them. This show of modesty and reluctance is all part of the ceremony.

If a Karen girl should die before she is married, she will always be buried in the skirt and seeded blouse of the married woman — borrowed from her mother if she did not have one prepared. The Karen believe that an evil spirit who would prevent the girl from passing safely waits on the road to heaven. But if she is wearing the clothes of a married woman she can say, "My husband is coming just behind," and the spirit will let her pass unmolested. Parents will journey any distance to change their daughter into the married woman's clothes if she should happen to die while away from home.

The Karen are the only tribal people to mark the change from unmarried to married status with such a complete and permanent change of costume.

The only other people to make use of seeds to decorate their clothes are the Akha. Job's Tears are used to make looped tassels for the sashes and headdresses of the women, fringes for the shoulder bags, and decorations for the cotton baskets that the women wear tied at the waist. They are also sewn in straight lines onto the jackets, and form a square around the applique on the back of the jackets made by the Yer Tung Akha. Many different kinds of seeds are also used for necklaces and are sometimes strung together to use as decorations on the woman's headdress and on shoulder bags.

Seeds are one of the natural resources of the hills which the Akha and Karen have put to good use. The stylised seed embroidery of the Sgaw Karen, occasionally seen also on Pwo Karen garments, makes full use of the shape as well as the positioning of the seeds for its effect, whereas the Akha are concerned only to string the seeds together for fringing. Both tribes, however, recognise the beauty of the smooth shiny seeds.

For necklaces and bracelets, the women string together many kinds of seeds of different colour, size and shape. Sometimes they add slender sections of bamboo, dyed pink for emphasis.

The Karen take a hollow grass reed, fry it to darken it to a deep brown or black, then chop it into short lengths and string these alternately with seeds.

It is important for Karen women to have something hanging from their necks, and usually they use seeds for this purpose. Even when they change to lowland costume they cling to their necklaces.

Dingles and Dangles

Akha headdress decoration

"Don't cover yourself up like that! You look like a corpse. The women and kids were frightened last night. The fringe of the blanket should be at your feet."

The anthropologist was very young and very keen. With only a perfunctory apology to his host, he reached for his notebook and recorded this new data enthusiastically under the section headed Taboos.

Goh-ouey had invited him to witness the annual offerings to the spirits of the family fields. Determined that his should be the definitive description of this important Karen ceremony, the anthropologist had brought with him a photographer and a prodigious quantity of notebooks.

The rice fields along the way were several shades of lively green. The soft rain seemed to make the young plants spring higher with every passing minute. It also made the narrow path as slippery as a wet fish. The soil was very porous from the last weeding. The anthropologist tried to steady himself by grasping at the rice plants, but they were too young to provide any support.

For the first time in his life, the anthropologist wished he could be a snake. He kicked off his mud-caked sandals in an effort to catch up with the tribespeople, who were walking quickly and steadily down the steep path, oblivious to the strong wind which threatened to wrench "Familial Relationships" from the precious notebook.

Suddenly the anthropologist's foot went numb. In a few seconds a burning, itching, searing sensation pierced his foot. Goh-ouey pointed nonchalantly to a small plant. "Elephant's Scream," he explained, and marched on.

At the field, Goh-ouey began preparing three leaf cups for the offerings. "The head of the family must do this," he explained. The anthropologist was confused. "Isn't the head supposed to be a woman?" He scribbled as he talked. Goh-ouey shrugged. "Sometimes." Into the cups he put cooked rice mixed with chaff, dried yeast, stems of pumpkin leaves filled with water, scrapings from tin bullets, leaves from all the plants growing in the field: corn, rice, tobacco and sesame. The photographer snapped frantically, struggling with his tripod and changing lenses under cover of a tattered umbrella.

Then the ceremony began in earnest. To the horror of the lowlanders, Goh-ouey, the shaman and his assistant began working simultaneously at three different points in the field. The shaman stuck a large tree branch into the mud. "Offering to Seng Fo and Seng Tai," he explained, smashing the heads of two large chickens, dripping blood onto the rice and decorating the leaf cups with chicken feathers. Against each cup he laid a small reversed ladder for the spirits to climb up.

The anthropologist was frantic. He slipped in the mud as he ran from one offering place to the next, shouting questions to the photographer and wiping mud from the notebook. The children, squatting by the side of the field, were convulsed with giggles.

Goh-ouey set up a platform with four stakes. "Offer-

ings to Dta-lue-meh and Hong," came the faint shout of the photographer. Meanwhile, the shaman's assistant split some bamboo stems to make cups for the rice whiskey and sacrificed a white chicken to Dta-seh at the third point. All three poured rice whiskey into a small container and placed this inside the leaf cup. Except for the shaman, who had a sip first. Did I see right, the anthropologist asked himself, scribbling illegibly in his book. The other two made the offering first, I'm sure of that.

Goh-ouey's wife (nobody seemed to take any interest when the anthropologist asked her name) began preparing the food underneath the field house. Evil-smelling smoke billowed from the wet firewood. Everyone helped to burn off the chicken feathers and to separate the innards into one container. Goh-ouey's wife started tearing vegetables into a pot, explaining it was not permitted to use a knife. She cooked the white chicken in a special pot and seasoned it with aromatic green herbs. The other chickens were added to the vegetables along with some salt and dried chillies. The sun was high in the sky but they had just started to cook the rice. The lowlanders were starving.

When everything was cooked the family mounted the crude ladder to the field house and seated themselves in a circle. The smell of the curries was irresistible, but there was one final ritual, explained the shaman: "First we must drink all the whiskey." The effect of the strong mountain brew on the empty stomachs of the lowlanders was overwhelming. They wondered how the children could stand it. When at last they were permitted to eat the curry, they felt too ill to enjoy it. And, they were told, the curry made from the white chicken, by far the tastier of the two, was only for the family.

After the meal, it was time for the divination. The shaman took two chicken thigh bones and stuck small pieces of bamboo in the holes. "If the bamboo pieces are in perfect alignment, the crops will be poor," explained the shaman, surreptitiously shoving one of the bones so that they were completely out of alignment. Everyone sighed. The result was favourable.

The anthropologist wanted nothing more than a long nap, but the family busily packed everything up. "We must leave immediately and not return for two days so the spirits can take the offerings undisturbed," explained the shaman.

As he left the field, the shaman lodged a slim stick into the middle of the path leading to the field hut, "to protect the lands from the wild elephant," he explained with an innocent, almost toothless grin. Then he burst into a song of rejoicing for the bountiful harvest to come and led the group on its long trek back to the village.

Now it was the shaman's turn to question. "Why do you want to know so many things?" The anthropologist wondered how to explain. "Because I want to record every detail correctly," he replied.

The shaman looked disapproving. "Anything too definite is not good," he said solemnly, and the family laughed.

Ya Khong Akha woman wears dangling ornaments even while working.

Meo girl with seashell necklace, a good-luck charm.

The next evening, the anthropologist took his notes to the house of the headman to ask for clarification on some points. The headman chuckled. "But who knows why things are done this way or that? Every family has a different ceremony. Even the shaman varies his actions every time. There is no single Truth!"

Hilltribe women take pleasure in an intense awareness of their bodies, and many costumes are designed to stimulate several senses at once. Their clothing reflects a close bond with nature, an attempt to imitate the flutter of a bird's wings, the rippling of a stream, the sparkle of dewdrops on a leaf.

Their use of colour is spectacular; their appreciation of texture is keen; but it is through an aura of constant movement that hilltribe women call forth the full dramatic and sensual potential of their costumes. Some garments,

notably the heavy pleated Meo skirts, are designed so that the cloth is always swinging and swishing about the body. In all groups, dangling ornaments are used as a charming fashion technique to create movement and to make each costume that little bit different from all the others.

Perhaps the most common of these ornaments is the necklace. It may be made from seeds, nuts, woven grass, lacquered thread or from the innumerable varieties of plastic and glass beads available in the markets. The possibilities are limited only by the ingenuity of the wearer and are subject to constant change according to the whims of fashion in the hills, so it is almost impossible to catalogue them with any accuracy. Necklaces are often worn in profusion, many different kinds mixed together, and frequently they offer the added dimension of sound. Strings of coins, the eyeteeth of tigers, bear claws, shells, fish teeth, small wasps' nests and silver bell buttons are especially eloquent.

The buprestid beetle, here shown on a bed of rice grains.

Completed singing shawl.

Strings of buprestide beetles for singing shawl.

Meo skirts swing seductively.

A Lisu man's courting finery: a set of colourful pompoms and an elaborate courting bag decorated with silver and tassels. Note lowland hairstyle.

Yao bride with part of her fringed veil pulled back.

Akha of Yer Tung group uses many dangling ornaments.

Pwo Karen unmarried girl's dress. Note fringe of silver bells under her arm.

Kayah woman with long fringed sash.

Lahu Nyi bag with many tassels.

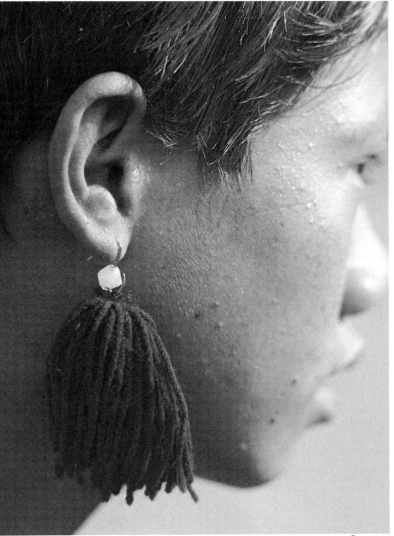

Lisu man's ear ornament of yarn.

Pwo Karen boy wearing a necklace of fish teeth. The name of the fish is yeh pleh.

Lisu man's ear ornament of folded grass.

Tassels offer another way of introducing movement, and they are used by most of the tribes. There are a few styles that seem to be peculiar to just one tribe. The Akha, for instance, make tassels from chicken feathers and fringes from loops of Job's Tears. The Yao like to wrap fine silver wire around strands of magenta-coloured silk, while the Lisu show a marked preference for a rainbow effect, mixing many different coloured yarns together. The Meo have a special liking for tassels of brilliant pink yarn, even adding them to the beanbag that courting couples throw in the New Year games. The Karen, Lahu Nyi and Lahu Shehleh twist the thrums, or last few centimetres of their weaving threads, into fringes that dangle from their shoulder bags. But there are many exceptions to these general rules. Tassels are popular and subject to frequent experimentation, so style, size, colour and location are variable.

The long tassels worn by both men and women of the Lisu tribe are more complicated than those of any other tribe. Each strand of the tassel is made from a length of cord approximately 50 centimetres long covered with tightly sewn cloth. Many different colours of cloth are used and each strand is finished with a tiny soft wool pompom in a contrasting colour. Like many hilltribe women, the Lisu like their stitches to be part of the decoration so they always work with thread of a different colour from the cloth. Working very fast, a woman will be lucky to make 10 of these strands in a day. As each complete tassel requires two sets of tassels, the whole process may take

Married Pwo Karen woman from Hot district wearing lacquer thread bracelets, bone-bead necklaces.

several months. Every member of the Lisu tribe must have a complete new outfit every New Year and the women begin the long task of making the new tassels as soon as they have finished celebrating the last New Year. A generation ago, the tassels were much sparser, but now it has become a matter of prestige to have them splendidly abundant — an average of at least 200 strands.

The two sets of tassels — the Lisu call them "belts" — are sewn onto either end of a 15-centimetre strip of cloth and worn over the sash. The men's tassels, which are slightly shorter than the women's, hang down the front of their costumes, while the women wear theirs down the back. The end result is not only brilliant in colour and seductive in movement, but it also offers the women the practical virtue of camouflage during menstruation.

Unmarried Pwo Karen girls make traditional and carefully regulated use of tassels. Their white dresses are usually decorated with fluffy red tufted designs across the shoulders and from knee to hemline. However, for ceremonial occasions the girls add a fringe of bright red tassels made from woollen yarn which hang from above the waistline almost to the hem, front and back. Funerals are the most important festivities for the Pwo Karen, and it is not uncommon for a youth to be heard sighing longingly: "I wish there would be a funeral!" Funerals are the only officially sanctioned occasions on which Pwo Karen can go courting, making them a time for dressing up and for making new friends. These long red tassels are a required part of the finery.

Pwo Karen girls have special "singing shawls" to add to their funeral-going costumes. When the young girls gather around the bier to sing the soul of the deceased to the afterworld, these shawls sway and swing. They are worn like stoles and decorated with hundreds of tiny buttons and pearly beads. A rippling fringe of iridescent green wings of the buprestid beetle adds glamour to the mourning. These stoles are unique to this tribe, and are now made in only a few remote villages. Many Pwo Karen have never seen or even heard of them, though they were once the finest pieces in any Pwo Karen girl's wardrobe.[19]

The Yao bride has another unusual addition to make to the gay world of tassels. Magenta-coloured silk tassels are fastened under the ruff at the back of the bride's tunic. The tassels are accompanied by clusters of silver bells, and cord made from several strands of silver wire twisted together; this intricate 'web' decorates the bride from her neck to the middle of her back. As her head is covered by the massive bridal headdress with its heavy fringing, the tassels down her back appear as an extension of the swaying screen that envelops her.

Although many of the most spectacular dangling ornaments are made of silver (and are therefore described in Chapter 12), many of the tribes have created unusual and often spectacular effects using less expensive materials.

Headdress

WE ARE PROUD of our fair skin and our raven black hair. We love to wash in the stream, and never cover our heads the way other tribes do.

Even if you search in seven hills you will never find a cleaner people, and in seven valleys you will never find a better place to live. Our village is near a crystal-clear stream bordered by huge trees that attract thousands of birds. It is two full days' walk to the nearest town.

We women love to bathe together, especially when the thin evening mist begins to set in above the river. But last night our pleasure was ruined by the mournful cry of a Great Hornbill which flapped frantically back and forth along the banks of the river, searching for its lost mate.

The pathetic cries pierced the hearts of everyone in the village, but for me there was a special sadness. The lowland hunters who stared so rudely at us while we bathed had presented me with the Hornbill's mate to cook for their dinner.

When they appeared in the village, they proudly showed their trophy to everyone, seemingly unaware of the horror hanging in the air. The lowlanders are so smart; surely they know that the splendid bird, its black and white feathers dropping and smeared with blood, its heavy beak gaping open, had a mate who would starve to death in mourning for her lost husband! Isn't there a blessing at every wedding ceremony: "May you love each other like the Great Hornbill"? Even the cruelest people in the hills refrain from killing the Hornbill.

Cooking for my guests is my pride and my pleasure. But there was no joy in it yesterday. I lingered long over my hair washing, letting it flow along with the current like an aquatic plant. I didn't want to face those lowlanders with their powerful guns and their stony stares which made me feel quite chilly.

Finally, I combed my hair and tied it into a neat bun at the back of my head. I had never seen the mushrooms the hunters had given me to cook with the bird stew. We eat many kinds of wild mushrooms, but these—well, these town people are smart. They must know what they want to eat. I washed the mushrooms slowly and took them to my kitchen.

The laws of hospitality take precedence over all else, and I cooked our highland rice by a special method. First I soaked it in boiling water, then steamed it in a wooden barrel. Finally, I simmered it in a deep pot. It was particularly tasty, fluffy and aromatic, a meal by itself and a perfect complement to the pungency of the bird and mushroom stew. For my beloved husband, I set out our basic dish of pounded chilli and salt, for I knew he would never touch the stew.

The hunters sprawled contentedly around the fire, complimenting one another on their hunting skills, swapping dirty stories and drinking our rice whiskey. By dinnertime they were quite drunk and very hungry.

I served them quietly, being careful to keep my eyes downcast just like any dutiful hostess of our tribe. They ate hugely.

When the first man knocked his head on the plate, we thought he had drunk too much rice whiskey. But seconds later a second man bit convulsively down on the spoon as he shoved a huge piece of meat into his mouth. The greenish colour of death swept the faces of lowlanders seated around our low dinner table.

The mushrooms! My husband leaped up frantically to search the shelf hanging over our fire for the dried turtle's head which we grind up as the antidote to poisonous plants. It wasn't there.

He rushed to the shaman's house, but although they turned the place upside down, that miserable little turtle's head was just nowhere to be found. I knew my husband wouldn't find it. When we married I chose to give him the pet name "awkward" which suits him perfectly.

After the men cleaned up the house and laid out the bodies of the hunters, my hair smelled like dried fish. I love to bathe in the river in the cool of the evening anyway, but last night it was particularly welcome.

There was a burning brand on the bank. The shaman's wife, my childhood friend, was already there. She let her hair flow along with the current like an aquatic plant, just as we used to do when we were young girls. How comforting to have company when you wash your hair at night.

The Akha woman's headdress is perhaps the most elaborate of all hilltribe headgear. There are many variations, the first of which is the baby's tight-fitting indigo homespun cotton cap worn pulled down over the forehead to eye level. It is decorated according to individual taste, but all caps contain the same basic ingredients: buttons, coins, feathers, tassels, fur and maybe some strings of Job's Tears. Young girls and boys wear a cloth cap of indigo homespun, lightly decorated with buttons, coins and feathers.

Girls change to the older woman's headdress at about age 12, with the onset of menstruation. As they get older, so their hats become more elaborate, until the decorative "peak" is reached around the time of marriage. The simple cloth cap will by this time have been replaced by a hat with a fitted headband at the front, and further back on the head, a high conical palm stem framework. The headband and chinstrap will be encrusted with silver (or aluminium, depending on the wealth of the family) half-sphere studs and fringed with silver coins that lie across the forehead and may also dangle in strings down the side of the face. The conical piece may be decorated with an impressively long list of possible ornaments: dyed bird feathers, squirrel tails, luminescent green beetles, beads, cotton or silk tassels, bamboo bands covered with grass stalks, various kinds of seeds, small shiny gourds, fresh flowers, tiny corked glass vials of perfume bought from traders, small booklets of coloured paper, and even sea shells which traders bring from the coasts of Burma and China and which generations of Akha women have prized as a special decoration. Most hats will be crowned with gibbon fur. The gibbon is becom-

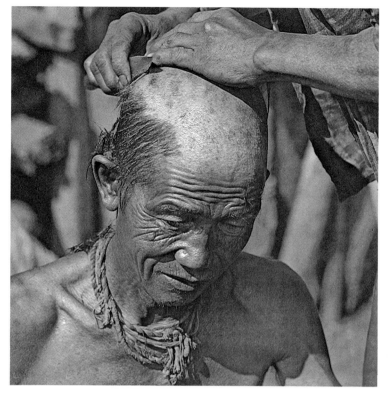

Lahu Shehleh man has his head shaved. In traditional fashion, he will reserve a topknot.

White Meo woman with hair cut short in front.

ing rare but dog's fur looks almost the same and is often substituted. Another very common decoration is chicken feather tassels made by detaching the barbs of the feathers from the central shaft and stringing them on a piece of thread to create a "bottle brush" effect. These tassels are usually dyed red or hot pink and hang in clusters around the sides or back of the hat. The height of these headdresses is a sign of wealth, and prosperous women like to build their headdresses very high for all the world to see their status.

There are, of course, many variations according to area and wealth. The women in one Akha group on the borders of Laos distinguish themselves by hanging waist-length tassels from their hats, each tassel weighted down by a silver ball three centimetres in diameter. Perhaps the wealthiest of all the Akha groups in Thailand lives in the far north in the village of Pa Mee. Here, the headdress of a woman may weigh as much as four and a half kilograms. The back of the headdress is covered with black cloth to which hundreds of tiny silver half-sphere studs, coins and other ornaments are sewn. A band of silver about three centimetres wide goes around this trapezoid-shaped back piece, and holds it to the rest of the hat. The crown is completely covered with tiny silver studs. Beads, ornaments and coins cover the flaps at the sides.

The Yer Tung Akha also have a particularly spectacular headdress. Married women attach a hollow silver back plate to their hats, usually about 25 centimetres high and about 13 centimetres wide, narrower at the top than at the bottom. This silver plate with its delicately beaten designs gives a rather angular look to the head; the effect is impressively prosperous.

A girl begins collecting silver pieces for her headdress about the age of 13, and parents often contribute to the collection as part of her dowry. Some girls keep their cloth caps as long as possible to proclaim their modesty and disinterest in men, while others can't wait to change into the headdress that will announce their readiness for marriage. Whatever their inclination, all Akha women are wearing the tall headdress by the time they are 20.

For her wedding, an Akha girl changes into a wide coolie-style hat for part of the ceremony. It is made from rattan finely woven onto a bamboo frame and lined with leaves or bark. Compared with everyday headgear, this hat is very plain, but it is gracefully shaped and most becoming to the young bride. Hats of similar shape but covered with jungle palm leaves are worn in the rice fields as protection from sun and rain.

The headdress of Akha men is much less brilliant than that of the women, for when they bother to cover their heads at all they sport nothing more exciting than a narrow black padded turban, worn like a tonsure. The trailing end piece is sometimes decorated with feathers and at courting time other decorations may appear: silver ornaments, tassels and fresh flowers. For many Akha men, the hair is more important than the headdress, for they shave their heads and leave one long top-knot. Without this, they believe they will go insane. According to one observer, cutting off this hair is "equivalent to the death penalty for an Akha man . . . for the psychological effect can be enough to drive him out of his mind."[20]

The indigo turbans of the Lisu and Yao women are large and well-decorated, and signal the transition from childhood to adolescence. All Yao children wear indigo cloth caps, not unlike the simple cloth caps of the young Akha girls in shape, but very differently adorned. Yao boys' caps have a narrow strip of embroidery around the forehead, a large red or magenta-coloured pompom on top and smaller pompoms around the head. The girls' caps are decorated quite differently. They have a band of embroidery in several different patterns which may be up to ten centimetres wide. On the crown there is a circular ruffle of red or magenta yarn with a big pompom over each ear. Sometimes silver studs and silver bells are added.

The expectant mother will make a hat for her coming baby, but only the forehead strip of embroidery can be completed before birth, for this is the only decoration both sexes have in common. The mother's ambition will be to make her child's head look like a flower, in order to attract a flower spirit to come and inhabit the baby, though the first child in the family is likely to be a more meticulously decorated "flower" than later arrivals.

As Yao girls reach their teens they begin to swap their caps for the six-metre turbans of their mothers and grandmothers. The long strip of cloth is usually only about 45 centimetres wide, and is embroidered at both ends with small individual patterns. A Yao woman is never seen outside her home without her turban, but she takes it off each night, often using it for a pillow, and rewinds it each morning before she sets off to work in the fields. There are several styles of winding and the way a woman wears her turban tells the knowledgeable observer just which area she comes from. It is a mark of good grooming, too, that no hair should ever be seen beneath this turban, so Yao women retain only a top-knot of hair and pluck all the rest — from eyebrows to high up on forehead and temples — by dipping two strings in ashes, twisting them around the offending hair and pulling quickly.

Although the heavy turban may show that a girl has reached marriageable age, it is not worn for the marriage ceremony itself. Instead the bride's hair is brought up through a tube in the centre of an oval piece of wood and "glued" into a fan-shaped arrangement with hot wax. A triangular frame is erected over this, with one leg attached to each end of the oval wooden piece and the third leg resting on the forehead. A bamboo trapezoid frame is fastened to the back of the wooden piece. This elaborate framework is then completely covered with a richly embroidered and tasselled cloth, and a plain red cloth covers the whole thing. The tassels are made of red or magenta-coloured silk and hang down so far that the bride's face can hardly be seen. Considering that the headdress has taken five laborious, not to say painful, hours to put on, this glorious shield may be a great relief to the weary bride. According to one very old Yao man, Yao women used to wear a modified version of this headdress every day, and it is only within the last 70 years that it has been replaced by the turban.

The bride is attended by three virgins who wear heavily embroidered and tasselled cloths over their turbans.

Yao men also have an interesting wedding headdress. Although they have adopted the beret for every day, grooms will still don the traditional red turban for their weddings, and, if they can afford it, will wear a silver "crown" over it. This consists of three flat silver pieces laced together with yarn at the corners. Many tiny fish-shaped pieces of silver dangle from the lower edge, and the silver is decorated with beaten and even cut-out designs depicting beings from the spirit world. The Yao are alone among the hilltribes in having wedding headdresses so markedly different from everyday wear.

For funeral wear, a Yao woman attaches a small piece of white cloth of her turban if she is a close relative of the deceased. The men wear a band of white homespun around their heads. This Chinese-style custom points up the close connection the Yao have maintained with their ancient homeland.

Lisu children, like Yao children, wear cloth caps when they are small but for the Lisu there is a pragmatic concern to protect small shaven heads from the sun rather than the interest in the flower spirits that the Yao hats reflect. Lisu caps are made from multi-coloured strips of cloth sewn together, topped with a pompom and adorned with tassels

Yao mother with her baby son.

Gue Ba Akha mother and child.

Akha of Ya Khong group.

Blue Meo baby girl's cap.

Yao girl's cap.

White Meo girl.

Lahu Nyi baby.

Yao baby boy.

Lahu Shi women from two different clans (opposite).

Young Akha girls of Yer Tung group.

Yao bridegroom's hat.

Yer Tung Akha woman.

169

Kayah women at New Year Ceremony, pouring lustral water.

Wieldng a bamboo spoon, this Lawa woman has decorated her head with an artificial flower and a long silver hairpin in her bun.

170

Blue Meo hairstyle incorporating a chignon of hair combings.

Sgaw Karen unmarried girl (top left) who has adapted the lowland hairnet for her headdress.

Lahu Nyi married woman.

Gue Ba Akha adolescent girl.

White Meo adolescent from Chomthong district, Chiang Mai.

172

Sgaw Karen married woman.

Headdress of 14 strips of checked cloth is held in place without aid of pins.

Young Lisu girls.

Sgaw Karen unmarried girls.

Lisu men's festival headgear.

Another style of Lisu women's headdress: plain black.

Yer Tung married woman (centre) with two unmarried girls.

Akha man's traditional headdress (top left) and thin braided topknot.

Pwo Karen bachelor.

over the ears. After the age of five, the children gleefully go bareheaded and it is an occasion for great excitement when the teenage girl gets her first turban.

This turban has a doughnut-shaped base of rolled cloth. Several metres of black cloth are wound tightly around this base and stitched into position so that the whole thing can be lifted on and off without rewinding. One end of the cloth is left loose and to this is attached a long tassel made of rows of multi-coloured beads, yarns, coins, sea-shells and pompoms. This tassel begins at one side of the turban, is stretched across the hole in the centre, draped gracefully around the front, passed under the beginning of the tassels again, and the last 30 centimetres are allowed to dangle down to the right shoulder. Unlike the Yao, Lisu women prefer to keep these turbans for dress-up occasions and do not cover their heads at all on ordinary days.

Lisu men have traditionally worn white turbans for festival. White towels have almost completely replaced the original homespun cloth because they hold their shape so well. The towels are doubled lengthways and a piece of cardboard is inserted as a stiffener. The resulting turban resembles a Russian astrakhan hat. It stands about 20 centimetres high and is wound so that the crown of the head is left bare. In the past, the men wore turbans made from 1.8 metres each of red, yellow, black and green or blue cloth, wound so that the end of each colour hung down the back. Some men still wear such turbans at New Year.

Blue Meo women usually wear little more on their heads than their enormous buns, padded out with hair-pieces concocted from hair combings. For special occasions they may appear in black and white plaid turbans, the shape and style of which depends on the careful folding and layering of 14 separate pieces of cloth. Flat silver pieces shaped like question marks go through the earring on either side, and the other end hooks into the turban at the back.

Young girls of the Blue Meo groups may wear a triangular shaped hat which has a stiff roll of cloth rising up from the forehead, and falls in zigzags of cloth to a small tassel hanging down the back. The sides of this unusual hat are usually embroidered and edged with brightly coloured cloth, which nowadays may even be some gay print that has taken the mother's fancy at the market.

The boy's hat, on the other hand, is a skull cap adorned with embroidered and tasselled earflaps and stiff protruding triangular "handle" at the front, thickly padded and covered with bright cloth. If there was once a significance to these distinctive styles it has been lost and only the stock response "because it's pretty" greets any questions.

When White Meo women dress up they tie their black turbans so that the cloth stands erect across the front of their heads and is supported by the large false bun on top of the head. A strip of embroidered cloth decorated with tassels, pompoms and coins is tied horizontally across the front of the turban.

Meo men and boys wear a skull cap made of shiny black sateen and topped wtih a large, brilliant pink pompom. Black turbans with embroidery and fringing at the ends are an alternative style. White Meo men often wear their hair in a queue.

Although the Karen like to keep their heads covered, believing "heads get cold but feet don't", head wear has always been simple. Traditionally, all Sgaw Karen women wore the *kopur khee* — a very narrow turban of white cloth with 30-centimetre red tassels at the end, worn so that they appeared at the front and were tucked into the side. Today, however, it is easier to use a market-bought towel. The very latest style is to sew beads into patterns on a purchased hairnet. And the men who once sported shiny red sateen turbans will now settle for any piece of market cotton, reserving the traditional turbans only for weddings. Pwo Karen men like to wear their hair in a queue, as do Kayah men.

Pwo Karen women save their hair combings and use them to fill an elaborate aluminium holder which they wear as a wig for special ceremonies.

The Lahu are not particularly interested in head wear. Lahu Nyi women tend to go bareheaded. Lahu Na women usually wear a towel turban and for festive occasions may wear a small plain black turban, allowing the ends to hang down their shoulders giving a veil effect. The men like to wear hand-knitted toques, or hats purchased from the market, but many appear in a black turban with long fringes on the ends for special occasions.

The Lawa, too, are quite unconcerned with headdress, but when they do cover their heads Lawa women choose a very thickly woven white homespun cloth, about 30 centimetres wide, which lies flat on the top of the head and is allowed to fall to the shoulders behind. This extra length of cloth can be folded onto the top of the head to provide extra padding when a woman wants to hang a laden basket from a strap across her forehead. On her wedding day, the Lawa bride drapes her head with white cloth. But for the most part Lawa women prefer to decorate their heads with sweet-smelling flowers. The men like to wear a small narrow turban made from any available cloth and wound in a rather haphazard doughnut shape.

The preferred hairstyle is fairly universal throughout the hills: hair is parted in the middle and caught up in a bun at the back. Meo women sometimes add tiny braids to their high coiffures. No tribeswomen ever part their hair on the side.

For some tribes, headdress is an all-important part of the costume, a necessary accompaniment to everyday life. For others it is part of their festival regalia, a sign that they have dressed specially for the occasion. And in all tribes, it receives far more attention from the women than it does from the men.

Silver Work

Yao single neck ring.

FU SENG squats on his small wooden stool, pumping the cylindrical bellows with one hand and peering at the silver in the heart of the fire. The liquid mass seems to change shape as he watches, pulsing with a life of its own.

The smith stares at it, bemused. For a long time now he has felt some force besides himself at work in shaping the silver. He is almost afraid to lift the new piece out of the fire, for fear that this time that force will be too strong for him.

The sound of his wife moving around inside the house breaks the spell and he shakes himself out of his reverie. He lifts the silver out of the fire with long-handled tongs and begins shaping it with his hammer, turning it deftly this way and that to get the metal even. Under his practised hands, a flower takes shape, scalloped edged, slightly concave. It is really a buckle, practical and almost prosaic, but it has a pleasing, graceful form. He has heard it called a "moon flower", a pretty name for a pretty piece.

Gradually hs feels the power of the silver begin to exert itself. The flower seems to move in his grasp, and he drops the hammer and grips the tongs with both hands, willing it to submit to him. Again the advice of his old teacher rings in his ears: "You must leave a flaw in each piece you make. If you insist on perfection, the evil spirit is trapped inside and will continue his evil work."

The smith glares in desperation at the flower he has made. He is holding the tongs so tightly now that his hands are shaking and the flower seems to writhe before him. He feels it mocking, daring him to try that one stroke out of alignment that will release the spirit.

He cannot give in. Never once has he obeyed the old belief and made a "gateway" for the spirit. Every piece he has made has been unmarred, an object of perfect symmetry, perfect beauty. It has always been a matter for pride. It is fast becoming a matter for fear. Every piece is harder to work now, every time the struggle threatens to overwhelm.

The buckle seems to be possessed by a life of its own now and the smith can hardly hold it. As he wrestles, drops of sweat run down his face and sizzle as they hit the glowing coals. His eyes narrow, staring at the tormented movements of his creation. As though in a dream he rises slowly to his feet and with a gesture of defiance, thrusts it back into the fire.

There is a hiss and the edges of the flower begin to dissolve. The smith watches all the distinctions disappear until there is only a soft, moving mass once more.

When he looks up, his surroundings are blurred. The world has become as distorted as the melting silver and he can recognise nothing. Everything is hazy, indistinct, somehow terrifying. He feels a power all around him, threatening, and he cannot stand against it.

He drops the tongs and gropes his way to the door. As he stumbles further and further away from his home, the coals of his fire slowly pale and the silver begins to harden again. But this time there is a gash on the surface where the tongs have struck – and stayed. The flaw is there at last, the gate open, the spirit free.

Three days later, a hunting party finds Fu Seng's body, torn and mutilated, lying in a ravine.

Although other Asian cultures prize gold, the hilltribes do not use it — except in teeth! Even if they could afford gold, it is questionable whether they would prefer it, for they find the weight, bulk and appearance of silver particularly alluring. They admire the qualities of gold jewelry, but as a point of fashion they feel silver goes best with their costumes. A piece of silver jewelry is usually large and highly visible, giving the wearer a feeling of owning something solid. Much of the jewelry they wear they have owned since childhood, and they regard it as almost part of their bodies. Indeed, when the Red Lahu make offerings to the spirits, they remove their silver jewelry and add it to the other offerings on the tray, to represent themselves. Naturally, they put it back on when the ceremony is finished.

Tribespeople may adopt lowland dress, but they will continue to wear their silver. They are reluctant to remove it, even when they have to stay in hospital. It has a sensual appeal for them. They like to finger their silver, taking pleasure in its cool, smooth feel. It plays an important role at social gatherings, not only because it denotes wealth and prestige, but also because of its decorative qualities. Tribespeople savour silver as a gourmet savours food, and at festivals they eye one another with a mixture of envy and admiration.

Silver has always been available in the form of coins, making it possible for even the poorest family to amass a collection of silver, one piece at a time. Indian rupees from the days of British rule and old French coins from Indochina have been the most common sources of silver. Traders travelling through the hills supplied these coins along with other necessities. More recently, silver ingots from China, imported to Bangkok through Hong Kong, are a more convenient alternative source.

In fact, Hong Kong silver fetches a better price than old coins at present in Chiang Mai. Indian rupee coins are only 85 per cent pure when melted, making them harder to work with than pure silver.

In some of the poorer villages, tin coins from Burma and Thai one-Baht coins are substituted on costumes or strung into necklaces.

Dowries of up to 30,000 Baht (US$ 1,500) have traditionally been paid in silver. Small silver "bullet" coins twisted onto a cotton string and worn about the neck were once the accepted currency among the Lawa and Karen. Silver jewelry has long been the most acceptable form of savings. Among those tribes too poor to buy silver, aluminium is used as a substitute and is beaten into replicas of the silver ornaments of the more affluent. Some of the tribes call this "aeroplane wing jewelry", for the first sheet metal used for this purpose was salvaged from planes that crashed in Burma during World War II. Today a more reliable source is sheet aluminium which can be purchased in lowland Thai towns.

A few generations ago, the tribes lived in almost complete isolation from one another and their styles and costumes remained distinct. They were also relatively wealthier, able to move freely through the hill areas that were almost unpopulated, and were thus able to ensure good harvests from almost virgin land. However, as populations have exploded everywhere, their movements have been greatly restricted. The land on which they are now forced to stay has become increasingly exhausted and their standard of living inevitably lowered. Their isolation has been encroached upon and their poverty deepened in a vicious circle of events from which it has been almost impossible to escape. As a result, less silver is being worked, and there are few skilled silversmiths among the tribes today. Formerly there would have been one in each village, but now one smith trades with all the tribes over a wide area, and is often reluctant to train younger men in his art for fear that their competition will threaten his livelihood. Canny silversmiths are also reluctant to train many apprentices. Apart from the headman the silversmith is likely to be the wealthiest man in the village.

Although a smith may be able to copy any tribe's designs, most of the tribes are now borrowing so freely from one another that it has become almost impossible to identify the design of any silver piece as traditional to any one tribe. Some of the traditional designs are being lost or interchanged with other tribes because poor tribespeople have been selling their jewelry in exchange for trade goods or to tourists for the last 20 years. Some of the silver now worn by tribal people is made by Shan silversmiths who have come across the border from Burma, and some of the oldest pieces can be traced to smiths in China. These influences have blurred tribal distinctions even further.

The silversmith is also almost the only source of credit for the tribesmen. He functions as a combination pawn shop, financial advisor, and gossip monger, and his house is usually the centre of inter-tribal transactions, which inevitably results in an extensive melting of styles. Because he is in contact with all the tribes, he himself may suggest changes in style, for he has all the latest information on what's fashionable.

Silver is cleaned once a year, just before the New Year celebrations. Most tribes rub their jewelry with ashes, then polish it with a cloth. Some Karens boil their jewelry in water mixed with tamarind or acidic berries, then rub it with strings of tiny high-fired glass beads brought from India by itinerant traders.

Because of the poverty in the hills, it is now becoming quite dangerous to wear silver jewelry for everyday. Most of the tribes like to wear some silver articles with their everyday dress, but whereas 20 years ago the full family collection would be worn everyday, it is now reluctantly

Shan belt and silver lime container.

kept safely stored away — perhaps buried in the jungle — and is seen only at festival times. It is intriguing to wonder how many such caches have been lost forever because accidental death has overtaken the only family member who knew the secret location.

Neck rings, buttons, bracelets, arm rings, belts, buckles and studs are among the most common everyday items. On festival days, necklaces with many pendant pieces, chains, earrings, rings, pipes and tobacco and betel boxes make their appearance.

All of these pieces are made at a simple forge by hammering and drawing — a process whereby wires are pulled through increasingly smaller holes until they are of the desired gauge. There are three methods for applying designs to a silver ornament. Chasing involves carving patterns into the silver with a sharp instrument. In applique, pieces of silver are "blown" onto the silver surface using flux and flame to cause cohesion. Repousse work pushes designs onto the silver by hammering from the reverse side. Moulds are also used, both for poured shapes and for hammered ones. In the production of the half-sphere studs, silver is pounded into indentations in a piece of buffalo horn. The mallets are also made from buffalo horn, because a metal hammer is too harsh.

Colour is not used extensively but the smiths do some enamel work on rings, pipes and pendants and an occasional piece is found that uses inlaid glass. Stones are extremely rare in hilltribe jewelry. The Yao language illustrates this lack of interest: there is only one word to cover all gemstones, and though they do differentiate jade and pearls with separate names, they neither value nor use them.

For several of the tribes, heavy neck rings are the first item in the silver collection. These neck rings are circles of solid silver which have a narrow opening at the back through which the neck will—just—pass. The opening is so narrow the neck ring has to be put on sideways. It is then fastened with a simple hook arrangement, but it is so difficult to get on in the first place that there is little danger of it slipping off unnoticed. Among the Meo, both men and women wear neck rings, and it is always the first piece of jewelry a Meo child acquires. A single ring is given to both boys and girls three days after birth and this ring is worn constantly. As the child grows the ring is melted down and enlarged with the addition of more silver. The Meo like to wear several of these rings of graduated sizes fastened together, sometimes as many as five at a time.

Neck rings are considered as individual as toothbrushes in Western culture, and are never "handed down" without being reworked and specially tailored for their new owners. A lost, stolen or sold neck ring apparently causes no spiritual anxiety, however. Only in times of sickness is it absolutely imperative to be wearing one's neck ring in order to survive, for the Meo believe that silver binds a man's souls together. Illness is a signal that the souls are threatening to leave, and the silver neck ring may hold them back.

The Yao also like to wear several joined rings, but the Akha, Lisu and Lahu prefer single rings, either the circle style or flattened rings with chased designs. If they have more than one they will wear them all together, usually all the time, even when working in the fields. Wealthy Kayah women wear a single solid circle of silver at the top of their lacquered cord leggings.

A common ornament on the everyday dress of the Lahu and Yao is the large buckle used to fasten the front opening of the jacket. These buckles may be of disc or rectangular shapes, almost always with delicately chased or hammered designs. The disc buckles are slightly convex, with a hole in the centre through which a tiny circular piece enters to close the buckle and at the same time forms the centre of the "flower" design. To this small centre-piece are attached two pieces of wire whose looped ends are sewn into the cloth. The edges are often scalloped. The rectangular buckles have hooks on one side that fasten over loops of thread on the other side of the jacket.

The largest disc buckles are those of the Lahu Nvi. One Lahu man commented with a merry twinkle that Lahu men like to tease their women by trying to touch their breasts and that women have retaliated by wearing larger and larger buckles, until some can now be found that are as large as dessert plates. It is more usual, however, for two or three smaller ones to be used to fasten the front of a woman's jacket. Akha women follow the same cus-

tom—though not, perhaps, for the same reason!—and Akha men wear them also, especially bachelors. Lahu Na women use smaller discs, while the Lisu sometimes add rectangular or disc style buckles to the profusion of silver ornaments decorating (rather than fastening) the black vests they wear over their tunics on festive occasion. Yao women use several small rectangular buckles to fasten their tunics, sewing them under the ruff so that they are hardly visible. Meo women do not wear them at all, apparently preferring to fasten their jackets with the more mundane safety pin which they feel offers greater convenience for breast feeding.

Both men and women have a wide variety of buttons to choose from. Jackets are often fastened with small hollow balls which have a thin piece of metal inside to provide a tinkling sound. These are favourites with most of the tribes. Other types of buttons are used more for decoration than for securing garments. Silver coins with a hole bored in one edge are widely popular. The Lisu like to use the small half-sphere studs to cover their vests with an almost solid screen of silver, with rows of coins and buckles for variation. The Akha and Lahu also use these half-sphere studs, but usually in rows around the edges and sleeves of their jackets or clustered in triangular groups of three. Lahu Na women like to mass them on their tunics in front or back. When Yao women use them they sew the studs into solid V-shaped designs along the tops of their New Year aprons. It is interesting to note that the Yao of the Chiang Kham area maintain that these "aprons" are really baby carriers and consider the custom of wearing them at the front as an apron to be a slightly absurd innovation of other groups who want to show off the decorations.

The aprons also have a religious function, for women use them to receive anything handed to them by the priest. And at the impressive "initiation" ceremony of the Yao, women use their aprons (and men the loose bottom edge of their tunics) to catch the spirit stamps (ian) and merit-making certificate thrown by the high priest.

Hanging necklaces are reserved for special occasions, probably because they would tangle easily and interfere with the daily chores. However, they are popular with most of the tribes. Most designs feature a chain with a selection of pendant pieces, but unlike Western styles the chains are not always fastened around the neck. They may be attached to another piece of jewelry — usually the neck ring — or, in the case of the heavy Yao back chains, to special loops sewn into the shoulder of the jacket. Some chains, too, are fastened only at one end and allowed to dangle to the waist, the end tucked casually into the belt.

There is wide variety in the shapes used as pendants on these chains. The Meo like to wear a small silver padlock which they believe will protect them from evil spirits. The Lisu like to wear a butterfly because, some say, it can fly anywhere and epitomises freedom. The Meo believe that the soul in heaven takes on the shape of a butterfly, but despite this — or perhaps because of it — seldom use the butterfly motif. The fish is another very popular motif, particularly with the Akha, who believe that if they dream of fish it means they are going to get money. For other tribes it represents simply good luck and undoubtedly also retains some of the traditional long life, prosperity and abundance symbolism attributed to it by the Chinese.

Bells, medallions and flower shapes are also used, but most common are the small club-shaped pieces which are usually grouped in large clusters. Lisu women in particular like these pieces, which they call flower buds, and will attach them to a choker-style appliqued cloth necklace in great numbers to form a heavy ruff of silver around their necks. The Lisu, using similar pieces, prefer to combine them with other shapes and will often wear them hanging down the backs of their costumes. Yao women also focus attention on the back by wearing elaborate back chains which may use many different shapes and often also include large silver bells. Club-shaped pieces are also suspended from the pendant necklaces and dangle from a wide variety of earrings.

Tribespeople who expose their backs to the crowd during dances and ceremonies decorate the backs of their costumes. The Karen tend to concentrate all their decoration on the front. Both the Karen and Lawa tend to use less silver than the other tribes. When they dress up they will don various kinds of necklaces, sometimes chains, sometimes coins strung together. Both tribes still use the old bullet coins, twisted onto strings, as necklaces. Kayah women use these bullet coins on strings as anklets.

On some of the pendant necklaces are found small tools, ranging from tweezers for that bothersome hair in the nose to "diggers" for getting at the wax in the ears. Other tools include head scratchers (particularly useful for those who wear wigs), nail cleaners and toothpicks. Other implements — like the miniature knife — have no practical purpose, but tiny silver boxes are sometimes used for carrying small amounts of balm or snuff, and some women add silver needle cases. This custom would seem to place these necklaces in the category of "functional" rather than purely decorative.

Repousse work on tobacco box.

Kayah necklaces of coins.

Lahu Nyi buckle.
White Meo rings.

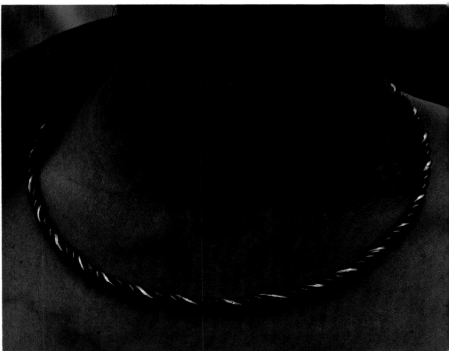

Meo spirit necklace of three strands of twisted metal.

Akha rings.

185

Lawa buffalo horn and silver pipe.

Yao silversmith at work.

Kayah horn and wood pipe trimmed with silver.

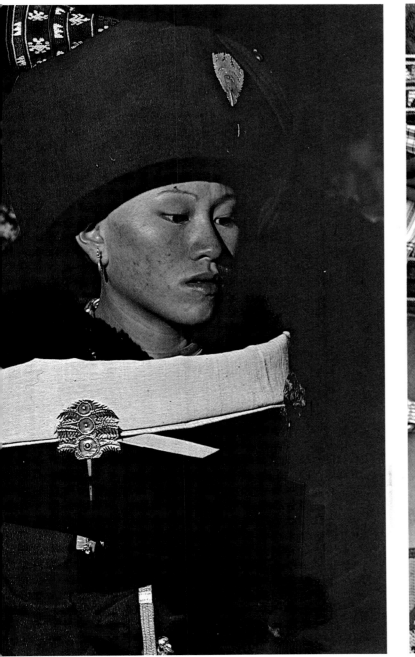

Yao bride wearing silver wedding flowers. *White Meo earring.*

Yao bridesmaid holds up backpiece for bride's costume.

Pwo Karen: only the teeth are gold.

Kayah finery: Note heavy earrings.

Neckpiece made by Shan silversmith, using enamel work on fish.

Hanging ornament from Shan silversmith. Note cylinders at top of centre ornament for keeping perfumes or powders, and also profusion of small practical tools.

Lahu earrings with chased design.

Padlock-style neck ring for Meo man.

191

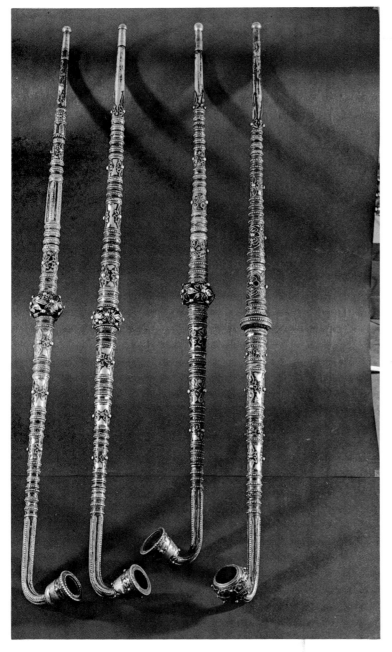

Silver pipes of Shan origin. Akha bachelors carry these and tobacco boxes when courting.

Karen bullet coin necklaces.

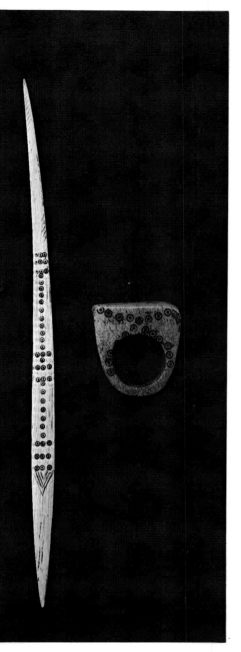

Karen ivory ring and hairpin.

Silver bracelets belonging to Lahu Shi refugee.

193

Akha woman getting ready for New Year swinging ceremony. Note silver studs.

Lahu Nyi girl with silver buckle.

Meo joined neck rings.

Wearing three belts is not unusual at a festival (Meo).

195

Finger rings are less popular with the hilltribes than with most other cultures, perhaps because tribespeople work so much with their hands that rings would be an encumbrance. The Karen wear a plain silver band ring for dress, and the Yao like to wear a similar one enlivened with strips of coloured enamel. The Meo have a saddle-shaped ring of beaten silver which is seen only at New Year. Several tribes, the Akha in particular, have a conical man's ring built up from overlapping silver loops and topped with a tiny silver ball. The female version of this ring is flat. Today either sex may wear these rings. None of these rings are particularly intricate or even beautiful, but they represent the extent of hilltribe concern over finger decoration. When hilltribe people do wear rings they tend to wear them in abundance, some on every finger.

Most tribal women have pierced ears and impressive dangling earrings to wear for festivals. When a child is very young the ears are pierced with a large sewing needle and a piece of thread is inserted. As the girl grows older, "keepers" of polished wood or even bone may replace the thread. It was once traditional among the Sgaw Karen women to wear circular earrings shaped like miniature funnels. Tiny ones were inserted into a girl's earlobe at about age 10 and gradually replaced by larger ones as she grew, until, at adulthood, her earlobes were greatly enlarged and able to accommodate earrings 2.5 centimetres in diameter. These earrings were once forged from Indian rupees for every woman in the tribe, but the custom has now died out in all but the most remote villages.

Applique work on bracelet found in Meo village.

Lawa hairpin with semiprecious stone.

Detail of Lahu Na finery.

Some Lawa women have borrowed this style. Kayah women also admire enlarged earlobes and they like to hang many solid silver pieces from their ears as weights to achieve this effect.

Both Yao and Meo women wear small sickle-shaped earrings as part of their everyday dress. As these are frequently required items, the smith usually keeps on hand a supply of silver pieces moulded into the shape of tiny swords. As earrings are requested he twists the "sword" into half-circles, rounds the edges, and twists the "handles" into decorative curls. The tip of the sword is now ready to slip into the ear.

Some tribes wear far more elaborate earrings on special occasions. Lahu Na girls favour a dangling style using clusters of the same club-shaped pendants that they use in their necklaces. Lisu women put a relatively small silver ring through their pierced ears and decorate it with a pom-pom. For dress occasions they link these earrings with several strands of silver chains which pass under the chin. Girls of the Lahu Shi group, on the other hand, wear an apostrophe-shaped earring made of drawn silver wire for dress, replacing similarly shaped wooden or bamboo ones worn as keepers every day. Some of the prettiest earrings include miniature copies of the shapes worn on the pendants, supported by tiny chains and fringed with many tiny silver dangles. Most of these earrings have less to do with tribal tradition than with the whim of the wearer and the skill of the silversmith; the variations are endless.

KAREN SONG

The spoon with the golden handle
The girl is the rice and the boy is the curry.
The spoon with the golden handle
The girl is the curry and the boy is the rice.
The girl and the boy love with the devotion
*   of the white heron.*
When you cut down the tree, the tree does not want
*   to part from the stump.*
When you say goodbye, I have no happiness
*   in taking a bath or washing my hair.*
I lose my appetite. I just cannot find any joy in living..
I cry until my eyes hurt.
When I do not see you for a day, it seems like ten days.
And a month is like a hundred years.
Don't go yet; come and live with me and help me
*   to farm the rice fields.*
You are like the corn in my life; come with me
*   and comb your hair nicely.*
You are like the rice; come with me and comb
*   your hair nicely.*

— Sgaw Karen Song

Although earrings are mainly a feminine ornament, Lisu and Lahu men like to wear a single silver earring dangling from the left ear as part of their dress costume, and both Karen and Lawa men pierce their ears and wear cylindrical ivory earrings. In the past, Karen men sometimes wore large cylindrical silver or ivory earrings, but this custom is now dying out, possibly because the elephant is becoming rare and ivory consequently harder to find.

Some bracelets are worn all the time. Karen bracelets, for instance, are part of everyday wear. One type is thin and twisted, sometimes coiling so many times that it may extend over 10 centimetres of the arm. Another type is a plain brass ring which is worn on the lower arm. A hill-tribe woman would never part with this bracelet because it helps to hold the body's spirits in place, and keeps evil spirits from entering. The Meo also have a "spirit" bracelet, but theirs is twisted from three strands, one each of copper, silver and iron. Tribes which are very poor may use a piece of cotton cord to represent this bracelet. When a person dies, this cord must be cut in order to release his soul. These may be worn around the ankle, arm or neck as protection against the most feared of their spirits, Bonsong. This spirit takes the form of a little girl with long hair who has an insatiable craving for fresh meat. Bonsong usually steals one of the souls wandering around the netherworld waiting for reincarnation, turns it into a tiger and sends it into the forest to do her killing. If she cannot find a soul, her desire for fresh meat may drive her to suck a human heart dry instead. Needless to say, these bracelets are worn all the time.

There are many other styles of bracelets to be found, and tribal women often wear them in profusion. Semi-rigid bracelets of beaten silver, sometimes as much as five centimetres in width, are popular with Lisu and Lahu Nyi women. Lahu Na and Lahu Shi women are more often seen sporting rigid, narrow bangles made by pounding the silver into a mould, then soldering the ends together. These bangles are decorated with small, pearl-like knobs, a style which originated in Burma. Kayah women wear a similar solid bracelet but it is left open so that it can be slipped around the wrist.

Yao bracelets are flat silver, about one centimetre wide in the centre, tapered to a narrow width at the ends and fastened with hooks and rings. They often have a heart-shaped piece dangling from each end, and are decorated with chased designs. Women of the Akha and Lahu tribes like to make their own bracelets out of long pieces of silver chain wound around the wrist to a width of three to five centimetres. Other bracelets are made like springs, and yet others are rigid, heavy twisted silver. Men like to wear bracelets too. A plain rigid band bracelet, sometimes circular, sometimes a broken circle, is the most popular masculine style, but thick bracelets shaped like dragons, each end being a dragon's head with a ball in its open mouth, are sometimes seen. These are either solid silver or hollow, and are most likely of Chinese origin, though Shan silversmiths in Fang District, Chiang Mai, are now making similar ones. These bracelets nearly always come in pairs, one for each arm.

One of the oldest of the silversmith's arts is hollow work. This is still being done, notably in the making of some Meo neck rings. The silver is shaped over a wax model and the wax is then heated to a liquid state and poured out. After the opening is sealed, a hollow silver ring remains. However, evidence of the method used is always visible, for the opening has to be closed from the outside. Old examples of hollow jewelries show no trace of such work, and their perfectly smooth, sealed surfaces are a puzzle today. The smiths say there is no one among them who knows the secret.

An unusual use for silver is seen in the Yao wedding flowers. These are made from thin sheets of silver, sometimes flower-like, sometimes more like little pine trees, which are given to the bride as wedding gifts. Each one has a long pin at the base, rather like an old-fashioned hatpin. The bride pins these gifts onto her headdress or sash as additional ornaments on her wedding day. These silver gifts represent a "nest egg" for the young couple, though most women prefer to keep them for sentimental reasons if possible. The Yao groom wears a "crown" of equally thin silver, decorated with punched and cut-out designs. (See Chapter 11 for a full description.)

Lawa women have a similar silver pin topped with a silver cone, but they use it to hold their hair in place only on festive days. Porcupine quills or bamboo pieces are substituted for everyday wear. Kayah women also like to wear a silver hairpin, similar in shape to that of the Lawa but less intricately designed.

Silver pipes and silver tobacco boxes are a luxury that every Akha man desires, for he believes that unless he carries them when he goes courting, he will not win a pretty wife and indeed will be lucky to attract any girl at all. Even if he has to borrow them, he must have them. The "tobacco boxes" are actually made for holding betel nut, and like the pipes, they are made by the Shans of Burma. Pipes and boxes of Akha manufacture are made of wood and bamboo. The only tribes which can be said to have their own silver pipes are Lawa and Karen. The Lawa pipe is made of buffalo horn curved almost into a U-shape and covered with tightly-wound silver wire. The bowl has a silver lip. The Karen pipe, a straight-stemmed style, is carved from wood with a flat strip of silver edging the bowl and another strip about one centimetre below the rim.

Wealthy Yao men like to trim their jackets with laid work of silver thread.

The poorer tribes, especially the Pwo Karen, use aluminium as a silver substitute. They also fashion their jewelry from copper and brass, in designs exactly the same as those normally worked in silver.

Silver tends to be the common denominator among the tribes. They all value it highly and use it as their decisive factor in determining wealth and status. Many items, notably the smaller ones like the half-sphere studs, are seen on the costumes of most of the tribes, and each tribe believes they are traditionally theirs. Certainly the way in which identical pieces are used differs with each tribe: single rows of the studs edging Akha sleeves, for instance, are very different in effect from the solid silver vests of the Lisu. But the item, the half-sphere stud, is the same in each case — except, of course, where aluminium copies are substituted. It is almost impossible to discover now whether one tribe invented it and others copied the idea, whether it was developed independently by several of them, or whether it was originally brought in by traders and sold to different groups who all devised different ways of using it.

Origins have long been a problem, and even among the most knowledgeable elders of the tribes no one can quite agree on when one style began, where it came from, or what it meant. Unfortunately, the problem is getting more complex almost daily, for as the tribes have increasing contact with one another, or come to share the same silversmith, the borrowing of styles increases. The influence of lowland style is important, too: some tribespeople have even begun to add gold necklaces to their jewelry collections. Wealthy tribespeople may hire a lowland silversmith to make their jewelry for them, introducing yet another opportunity for change. There is some confusion among the young people about which style of bracelet or necklace was traditionally worn in Grandmother's day. Like young girls everywhere, hilltribe adolescents are more concerned with what is pretty and fashionable. Lawa girls will gaily add, say, a Lisu necklace and a Karen bracelet to their best outfits if they can afford to buy them, much to the bewilderment of the outsider who is trying to identify silver by tribe. If these trends continue at the same pace, it seems likely that there will eventually be a complete blending of styles and very little will remain that is distinctive to any one of the tribes.

One factor ensures that silver will continue to be a favoured metal in hilltribe dress. If a father can dress his son or daughter in silver, it is his pride as head of the family, and sign of his ability to be a good provider.

In recent years, hilltribe jewelry has become popular with lowland Thais and tourists, and a great deal of silver jewelry can be found in shops in Chiang Mai and Bangkok. But 90 per cent of the "hilltribe" silver offered on the market is actually made by lowland silversmiths and smoked to give it a tarnished effect.

There are two major differences between authentic hilltribe silver and lowland imitations. On lowland jewelry, the lines will be clear and precise, while hilltribe designs have much more blurred lines. Usually a hilltribe silversmith will make, at most, three pieces the same. A sure sign that jewelry is of lowland origin is if the shopkeeper offers ten or more identical pieces.

Bamboo and Rattan Work

Kayah man playing bamboo pipes.

THE BAMBOO grove looks romantic in the pale light of the moon. A sudden gust of wind adds the pungence of fragrant wild flowers to the scene. Amijou watches thoughtfully, her fingers busy spinning cotton from the basket at her waist.

The courting ground (taekor) is active tonight. A group of men has just finished a vigorous dance and the dust is still hanging thick in the air. Amijou is not impressed with any of them. Ayoh is a widower. Alomah is too slick, with his fancy clothes and lowland mannerisms. The two nice-looking ones were out of the question because they are the sons of her uncle. And the other ones look like drunks or opium addicts. Amijou longs to succeed tonight so that she will have secrets to share with her girlfriends in the fields tomorrow.

She has washed her hair with rice juice to make it black. Her hair is parted in the centre and drawn across her face in an inverted V shape, just brushing the edges of her eyes. It covers her ears and disappears into the headdress at the back. Her costume is soaked in honey solution and perfumed with scented (miada) grass. Her spinster aunt, who is also a shaman, has given her a ball of charmed wax which she has in a section of her belt. Though she had never married because of a lame leg which made her undesirable as a bride, sharp-tongued Auntie was an expert in matters of courtship. But tonight it seems all their preparations will be to no avail.

Five girls come out to sing and dance near the fire. They cling tightly to each other as though compelled to give one another support. They sing –

De bor shor, lei de bor shor
skip and skip, skipping hurts my legs,
Skip, skip, and skip, I don't want to skip tonight
I have such a headache.

One by one they drift away from the dance ground with their chosen partners. Amijou begins to feel she shouldn't have come.

Suddenly a man walks out of the darkness and sits down at the next bench. He has a bulky blanket on his back with a flashlight hanging down from his shoulder and a knife at his belt. His dark jacket hangs open to show an abdomen as strong as a plank. Amijou's heart beats faster when she sees the indications of bachelorhood: nice silver buttons, gleaming silver bracelet. The man has shaved his head clean except for a small clump which hangs long and loose. In the light of the fire, she can see the stains of betel nut on his lips. His eyes shine like the eyes of a black snake. Here is a real Akha man.

The stranger starts to play his crude banjo with a tune she has never heard before. He must be from an out-of-the-way village. She tries to imitate the tune on her Jew's harp and giggles at her own failure. The man continues to play as if she doesn't exist. Amijou calls out imperiously: "Brother, your legs must be short and weak. You can't even move from there to here."

He drops his banjo and looks directly at her. Amijou lowers her eyes. The man comes over to her bench and puts his arm around her neck — and his right leg over her right thigh. He snarls: "I do have good long legs!"

Amijou had never realised that ordinary banana leaves could be so silky to lie on. The phosphorescence from the bamboo clumps around her bridal bed had paled considerably, and the roosters had stopped crowing. It must be late. How embarrassing! How could she make her way through the village? She lingered a few moments longer and picked some bamboo shoots. When she arrived home, she put them down on the shelf near the door. Her aunt called out from a dark corner in the house: "Za! Picking bamboo shoots at sunrise? I hope you got young ones!"

Amijou washed the dirt from her hands and shook them dry, hoping the gleam of the silver bracelet that she won in the bamboo grove would catch the eye of her spinster aunt.

Oh beloved stranger, you are so mean:
You've cut all the white bamboo in the village.
Oh beloved stranger, you are so mean:
You've cut all the bitter bamboo on the hills.

— White Meo song

From the day of his birth to that of his interment, bamboo plays a vital role in the life of a hilltribesman. When a child is born, its umbilical cord is cut with the sharp edge of a piece of split bamboo. Hilltribe tradition dictates that the placenta be buried in a bamboo joint. At the end of life, a shroud of split bamboo covers the tribesman whose family cannot afford expensive burial blankets. And bamboo groves mark the graves of rich and poor alike.

The first sight to greet any visitor to a hilltribe village is usually that of women of all ages carrying water in lengths of bamboo carefully balanced in bamboo baskets.

From the roof of the house to the smallest household utensil, bamboo is indispensable to the hilltribesman. It is a sure source of firewood no matter how heavy the rains, for the centre of the dead but not yet rotten stalks is always dry. It can be split into kindling, or, among the Lahu, shaved into tiny pieces to act as fuel in their cylindrical buffalo horn firemakers. It offers the best-known method of preventing the wanderings of a suicide's ghost, too, for 30-centimetres bamboo stakes driven into the body's heels are guaranteed to hobble the ghost.

Bamboo is a major source of construction materials, used for everything from houses to furniture to looms, and it is an important source of much of the hilltribesmen's pleasure, in such items as pipes, tobacco boxes and musical instruments. It is also an important source of food in the rainy season, when a major part of the hilltribe diet is bamboo shoots.

There are many varieties of bamboo to be found in the hills, and each has its own special function. One sort has tender young shoots suitable for eating. Another provides the hollow aromatic tubes in which *khaw laam,* a mixture of sticky rice, coconut milk, rice water and beans is steamed. The types with large, thick thorns make good fences, while others provide materials for roofing and flooring. Yet another bamboo strain is flexible and therefore good for making the low round tables used in some hilltribe households.

One variety of bamboo can be used for making twine because its fibre is more flexible than that of others. And one rare type is sought by Meo tribesmen for making their bamboo hardwood pipes. As if this were not enough, bamboo seeds are edible, tasting just like rice.

Houses with thatched roofs must have a long bamboo pole for the beam. For the Meo, it is absolutely imperative to place the tip of the pole at the roof joint and the base on the floor; otherwise the family will quarrel all the time. *Salas* or rest-houses near the village or in the fields, can be constructed quickly from bamboo. Lengths of bamboo are merely split in half and laid side by side for a quick roofing job.

Mats may also be made with bamboo where grasses are not readily available. When hilltribe family offers visitors a mat to sit on it is a mark of respect.

One of the most specialised uses of bamboo is seen in the Lahu crossbow. The stock is made from the wood of the chicken-blood tree, so called because of its red sap. The cross-piece is made of bamboo heartwood, which must be over two years old to ensure its strength and precision. In the very best bows cross-piece is made of wood. Where the cross-piece meets the stock, a small piece of cloth is inserted to allow the wood room to swell and shrink. The bowstring is made of twisted hemp, spliced back into itself rather than knotted at each end, and offers a maximum pull of 55-60 kilograms. The hunter usually has to use his feet to cock it, but because the string strikes the arrow rather than launching it, there is some loss of velocity. Nonetheless it makes a formidable weapon and one of which the hunter is very proud. It has a range of about 37 metres.

Every bow is lovingly carved and polished, and before it is used for the first time it is hung near the cooking fire for some weeks to absorb strength and fullness from the smoke, and extra polish from the spitting fat. The hunters

Pwo Karen bamboo stilts.

Blue Meo boy with horse pannier.

Bamboo-gourd pipe being played.

Meo back-pack basket.

Lahu Shi woman weaving basket for storing cooked sticky rice.

Lisu spirit shelf decorated with chains of bamboo "silver jewlery".

Kayah lacquered rice-whiskey cup.

Karen lacquered honey basket.

Lawa container for kitchen utensils.

Wallet and letter container.

Karen clothing storage basket of bamboo and palm leaves.

Yao bamboo spirit houses used specially in "initiation" ceremony.

Karen boar tusk and bamboo combs.

Lisu grass toys for
children (top). Left,
"horse" for boy. Right,
"bracelet" for girl.

Akha man's pipe and Meo Jew's harp (top).

Crossbow lying on low round dinner table (above).

Akha bird caller (above).

Akha bamboo-gourd pipe.

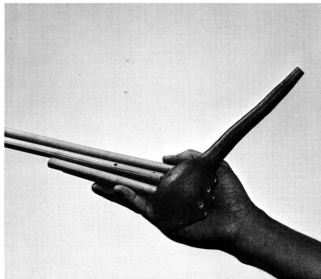

207

believe every bow is inhabited by a spirit and after each kill they dab some blood and some fur or feathers of the prey on the stock to encourage the spirit to help them hit the next target as well.

The arrows or quarrels, are also made of well-aged bamboo, cut to an oval, not round, shape and retaining the bamboo skin on one side so that it will slide more easily. The sides of the bow are also waxed to help the arrow slip. The arrows have no head, but for large game the sharpened tips will be dipped into a poison similar to curare, made from the sap of the *Upas* (Antiaris toxicaria) tree. A Lahu hunter has even killed an elephant with one cross-bow shot by sending one of these poison-tipped arrows into its trunk. Should a hunter wound himself with one of these poisoned arrows, the juice from young bamboo shoots will help to heal the injury.

The men of several other tribes, notably the Meo, also make crossbows, the only noticeable difference being that the Lahu set their horn or bone triggers into the stock, while the Meo attach a wooden trigger to one side. However, there seems to be considerable difference in the enthusiasm with which these hunters' weapons are wielded. The Lahu are the acknowledged masters of the hunt and in that tribe "the most respected man is the one who can claim the title 'Supreme Hunter', an equivalent in their society to the most esteemed of our PhDs, and a degree which is bravely earned. . ."[22] It is perhaps their eager aspiration to this title which makes them the greatest hunters in the hills. A Lahu father makes a miniature crossbow for his newborn son to ensure that the baby understands his role as a hunter and provider of food right from the start. For a baby girl he makes a tiny spindle.

All kinds of traps and snares for birds, jungle chicken and fish are also fashioned from bamboo. Some tribes build a corral from the white part of the trunks of banana trees, then throw stones into the water to chase fish into the traps. Others build a small dam, then drain the water out and harvest the beached fish.

Bamboo and rattan are used together to make many kinds of mats and baskets, woven by the men rather than the women. Only in the Lisu tribe do the women weave baskets, though the men prepare all the rattan and bamboo strips. Strips of bamboo usually form the body of the article, while rattan is used wherever there is a need for durability and flexibility. Thus the flat surface of the low round table used at mealtime is made of bamboo while its handles, base and corners are of rattan.

Rattan is also prized for its decorative function. The tribespeople dye it black by soaking it in water for a week or by dipping it in indigo, and brown by hanging it in the smoke of the household fire for a while. Patterns can be formed by weaving the darkened strips in with the natural coloured rattan strips.

Unfortunately, rattan is often difficult to find, for although bamboo grows almost everywhere, rattan requires a humus soil and lots of water. As the hills become ever more crowded, the forest diminishes yearly and there are fewer hospitable spots for the rattan to grow. In addition, the edible young tips of the rattan vine are a hilltribe delicacy. These tips are toasted to give them the aromatic and slightly bitter taste that the hill people like so much, and are just as likely to end up in someone's curry as in a basket! Rattan seeds, too, are edible. Some of the tribes in Thailand have almost stopped using rattan in their baskets because of the problems they are having in finding it.

However, baskets are still widely used in the hills to transport and store belongings, and they come in a great variety of sizes and shapes. Among the more unusual is the Karen clothes storage basket which is shaped like an inverted cone. It stands 1.2 metres high and tapers from a wider mouth to a narrow bottom, then widens again to flat, wide base. It is covered with a half-sphere lid. The Karen also make a cylindrical bottle-carrier basket, and a 2.5-centimetre diameter cylinder used for carrying messages. The Lisu and the Meo make sturdy oval panniers to sling on their horses. The Akha make a small rattan basket for carrying cotton tufts. It is very narrow and flattened at the base but opens to a wide round mouth at the top. The women tie it around their waists with cord. The Akha also make round bamboo and rattan rice bowls and large flat trays for family service. The Lahu Shehleh make square baskets with little legs for the same purpose. Round bamboo boxes are used by most of the tribes to carry or store such diverse articles as lunch, jewelry, money, sewing and tobacco.

Many old baskets have turned a rich brown after years of standing in the smoky interior of a hilltribe house. The smoke, incidentally, acts as a natural insect repellent. Baskets which have not been cured over the hearth fire are soon destroyed by insects.

Some baskets, such as those used to gather honey, are lacquered, and are deep dark brown in colour. However, this lacquer, from the sap of the *lac* (Rhus vernicifera) tree can cause rashes and allergies, and lacquered baskets were abandoned with relief on the appearance of plastic or tin containers. The Karen still know how to make lacquer, but they weave few baskets today, and the art of lacquer-making may soon be lost.

Small round stools, similar in design to the tables but without the surrounding raised rim and usually lacking the decoration, are made by the Lahu and the Akha and used by most of the tribes. Yao women can always be seen squatting on these low stools, a basket of embroidery threads beside them.

Bamboo shoot is an important source of food during the rainy season. There are at least 27 varieties of edible bamboo. Some types of shoot taste sweet, others aromatic. For immediate consumption, the shoots of most varieties are trimmed of their tough parts and then boiled twice for one hour. The water is discarded each time. Some sweet varieties, however, may require as little as 10 minutes boiling. To preserve bamboo shoots, hilltribe housewives may store the uncooked shoots in a salt-water brine, or in rice washing water. This latter method results in a form of pickle. In many tribes, the caterpillar that lives in young bamboo stalks is also a delicacy. The Akha eat two types, which they call the *kabue* and the *beetung*.

Lengths of green bamboo are used as cooking utensils to steam or bake many different kinds of foods, while dried bamboo provides most of the eating utensils. It is carved into cups and spoons, split horizontally to make

Bamboo slippers for Yao bride.

trough-shaped bowls for curry, or cut into strips and woven into plates. Green bamboo also provides spits for cooking large pieces of meat, and skewers for small ones. Sections are used as water carriers and containers. For aqueducts, a relatively luxurious invention, whole stems are split open longitudinally, placed end to end and supported with

Bamboo aqueduct in Akha village.

Akha man smoking bamboo water pipe.

forked sticks to form a long elevated trough.

Bamboo also provides almost the only toys available to hilltribe children. As the children begin to work hard at a very early age, they have little time for play. However Akha children have bamboo stilts and hoops, and the men sometimes plait tiny horses and buffaloes. Boys carve tops of wood, and girls can sometimes be seen nursing a large cucumber for a doll. For the most part, however, children seldom have toys, even simple bamboo ones. Nor do they seem to have anything soft to cuddle. A length of dry bamboo is used as a pillow, and all the blankets made in the hills are coarse in texture.

The gourd pipes and pan-pipes that provide most of the music in the hills depend on bamboo. Hollow stems of varying lengths and diameters are fitted into holes bored in one side of a gourd or hardwood resonating box. There are several variations in style and usage. The Meo play a bamboo-hardwood pipe while the Lahu, Lisu and Akha use bamboo-gourd pipes.

For the Lahu Nyi, the bamboo-gourd pipe is a woman's instrument, small and high-pitched. All the other tribes including the other Lahu groups, consider it a man's instrument. It is usually played while a group dances. In the Lahu Shehleh dance, the women cross arms and link hands, forming lines of three or four, and circle around the central fire of the dancing pen. The men weave in and out among them playing their pipes to give the rhythm. In the Lahu Nyi dance, women play pipes while the men beat drums and gongs. The Lahu are renowned for their ability to make their pipes "talk" and especially during courting they send messages from house to house, and even across the hills, with these pipes.

In the Lisu dance, rows of women radiate from the centre like the spokes of a wheel while the men dance in a circle around them. The Lisu pipe is made from a very long gourd with six bamboo pipes. Three pipes are topped with inverted "cups" and one ends in a bamboo crosspiece. Perhaps the most distinctive feature of this pipe is its low continuous drone note which, it is believed, goes straight to the Great Spirit. The Lahu Shehleh pipe is similar, with a lot of decoration on the top.

The Meo bamboo-hardwood pipe is an exception for the player always performs solo, dancing as well as playing. The dancing, a turning, dipping motion, is an integral part of the playing. First the performer leaps high into the air. Then he turns, bobs down and sits back on his heels to brace his body for another leap. The music goes on at the same time, its rhythm depending on the performer's breathing. The instrument itself is made of two hollow pieces of wood wrapped with brass rings to make it airtight.

Another bamboo instrument is the lovers' harp or Jew's harp made by many tribes to enliven their courting days. This harp may also be made of brass, and both sexes play it. Harps with a low tone are called "male" harps while those with a high pitch are known as "female" harps. However, either sex may play either type of harp. There are two other simple bamboo instruments. A primitive drum can be made with a good resonating length of bamboo, which is not beaten but merely pounded rhythmically on the solid ground. And a sort of instant banjo for children consists of a length of bamboo whose outer skin has been sliced to form the string. The whole segment forms the resonating box. Bamboo is also used to make flutes, bird callers, and cow and buffalo bell.

A variety of other musical instruments are made of wood. The Karen make a harp. The Lisu make a mandolin using brass wire for the strings and lizard skin to cover the wooden resonating box. There are various types of bells, drums made from logs with animal skin drum heads, banjos and guitars. Many tribes also use the buffalo horn, the Karen probably being the most skilled at making it. This horn is not so much a musical instrument as a signalling device, used to call people together, to signal that it's time for the tribe to go out and harvest the rice or to celebrate a wedding. The Yao use this horn during religious ceremonies to call up the spirits and also beat it rhytmically. During some ceremonies, pieces of paper stamped with the image of a horse are burned. The horse carries the message to the gods, and the rhythm produced by beating the horn helps to hasten the horse on its way.

Tubes for a myriad of uses are fashioned from bamboo, the most notable being the water pipe. This uses a whole section of bamboo, closed at both ends and having a small stem of bamboo inserted about halfway along. Tobacco, or even a cigarette, is placed in the small stem. The vertical large stem is half-filled with water, and the smoke filters up through the water to the smoker through a small opening at the top. Akha women make a more conventionally shaped pipe from bamboo and dye it pink. It is incised with designs, and decorated with buttons and coloured thread.

The Yao and Meo even make sandals from bamboo. After beating and soaking, finely-cut lengths of bamboo achieve a rope-like texture, and are woven into a thick-soled sandal. The strands are threaded through loops along the edges to form the "sides" of the shoe, and they hold the shoe in place when tied around the ankle. Although such shoes are stiff and rough when first made, they become very soft and comfortable with constant use.

Because it is so easy to work with, bamboo is also the material most commonly used when dealing with the spirits. Strips are woven into spirit houses, tables and altars. Tiny bamboo utensils are used to hold wine and food offerings. Bamboo strips are fashioned into "silver jewelry" and placed around the house or village to attract or appease the spirits. And in every Akha house, a bamboo joint topped with bamboo fibre contains the spirits of the family's ancestors.

The Thrums

Pwo Karen children guard an offering to the spirits of the rice fields.

The hilltribes and their handicrafts are inseparable. Much of their culture, heritage and tribal identity is expressed in their handiwork, and this gives the crafts an importance far beyond the value, or even the beauty, of any item. Although they belong to the realm of tradition, the crafts have never been static. Innovation has always been admired, creative imagination highly prized.

Perhaps this is just as well, for it is enabling the tribes to cope with a process of change that has become almost frighteningly rapid. Gradual change has always been inevitable because most of the crafts are highly perishable. Few of the articles survive more than a generation. Indeed, most of the clothes are worn until they disintegrate, and that seldom takes more than one year. Only the silver endures and even this is subject to periodic melting and re-working. In such circumstances, variations were expected and enjoyed.

But over the last 15 years alterations in the economic status of the tribes have introduced a new factor. Perhaps for the first time, the crafts are changing in response to influences from cultures other than those of other hill people. As a craft becomes a source of income, so it is adapted to the demands of the marketplace. Particularly noticeable are the modifications of colour to suit the tastes of new customers. Yao women, who traditionally use a large number of strong colours in every embroidery pattern, have learned to work with attractive but very un-traditional combinations of, say, red-white-blue or blue-green-purple because these will sell better. Many women are reluctantly learning to duplicate their work, although traditionally every piece was regarded as beautiful largely because it was unique. Meo women began to make their applique squares in patches (for pockets) or even sets (for dinner mats) when they discovered these sold much more readily than a collection of costume pieces which look unrelated (or unusable) to the outsider.

Some completely new products have also appeared. Lahu weavers now produce table runners and wall hangings on back looms that once made only shoulder bags. Yao embroidery can now be found on table-cloth and napkin sets, on spectacle cases and matching key chains.

There is also an increasing exchange of designs and techniques among the tribes, and though it is producing some interesting crafts, tribespeople are beginning to lose their identity as separate groups. Intermarriage or simply a desire to blend with lowland people has speeded up this process. An interesting situation in the Mao Chan area illustrates this "melting" process. Recently, a group of Lahu migrated into the area and settled near an established Akha village. They continued to weave their Lahu bags for sale to lowland shops, but soon noticed that the Akha bags made by their neighbours were selling better. It didn't take the Lahu long to realise the financial advantages of making Akha-style bags, and because Lahu weaving is firmer and the stitches finer, Lahu-made Akha bags are now more popular than the "real" thing!

Purists may contend with some justice, that the changes are destructive. Certainly some of the skills, such as the making of natural dyes, may soon be in danger of being forgotten. If an item is not marketable, the tribes will eventually stop making it.

On the other hand, the opportunity to experiment with new materials and unaccustomed colour combinations is stimulating a new wave of creativity. The old skills are being used in new ways. One example of this is the Meo batik. It has been tried on silk instead of homespun hemp and in various colours instead of the traditional indigo

blue. The designs and methods have not changed, though the purpose and the product are very different. And the results are pleasing to hilltribe eyes.

A small but interesting change is the growing interest in the textile crafts shown by the men. Over the last five years they have begun to work in a field that was once regarded as exclusively female. They have been experimenting with spinning, and some of the Akha men have even tried hand at embroidery. Ten years ago this would have been the laugh of the village but today it is becoming acceptable. In former times, the men spent their spare time making hunting equipment. With game scarce and money in short supply, they are turning to handicraft work from economic necessity rather than from choice.

Yet another positive result may simply be the continued existence of the crafts. As a source of income they are valuable to the tribes and therefore are unlikely to disappear even in the face of competition from ready-made goods.

However the case is argued, the process of change cannot be reversed. This book is a record of the crafts as they are, or in some cases as they have been: an attempt to provide some reference points in a cultural heritage that one day will be changed beyond recognition.

Golden Triangle village basks in the afterglow as a youngster prepares to leave the shelter of home.

Akha village gate.

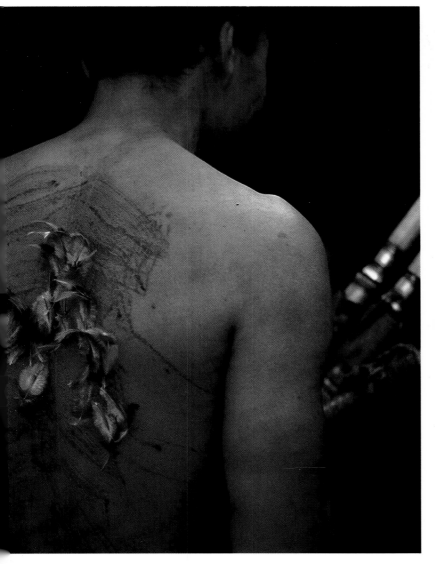

Naming a newborn child ceremony. The back of the name-giver is smeared with chicken blood and feathers.

Breast feeding in a Kayah village.

Kayah boy damping roof during field-burning season.

Buying a pig.

Gossiping at a Yao wedding party.

Weaving cloth.

The first ice cream.

Piggy-back ride (Lahu Shehleh).

Lisu girls playing hide and seek.

Lawa spirit offering of rice, burnt animal bones, cotton balls and a live puppy (top). Lawa hearth fire.

Dancing at night.

Dancing at dawn.

NOTES

1. Place names used in this book are spelled according to the Times Atlas of the World, Comprehensive Edition, 1973. Where towns and villages are too small to be included in that work, we have used the Thai Post Office official spellings. Please note that Mae Sai was formerly known as Wiang Phran and is so marked in the Times Atlas.

2. Peter Kunstadter, "Life among the Gentle Lua", *National Geographic Magazine* 130:1 (July 1966), p 141.

3. Population figures in this chapter are quoted from the latest available figures from the Tribal Data Project of the Tribal Research Centre in Chiang Mai. The figures were gathered between 1972 and 1975. It should be noted that numbers fluctuate according to tribal movements and that even in settled villages it is often difficult for population experts to gather reliable statistics because of the complicated extended family structure. In addition, recent political events have forced more tribespeople into Thailand and from neighbouring countries. Many of these, notably Meo from Laos, arrived in 1975 and 1976 and most are still living in refugee camps. All figures, therefore, must be regarded as approximate.

4. ————. Minority Groups in Thailand. U.S. Department of the Army. Washington D.C., 1970, p. 700. See also People of the Sun. John Blofeld. Hutchinson, London, 1960, p. 130.

5. Robert Morse, "The Lisu of Thailand", *Sawaddi*, Nov.-Dec. 1975, p. 17.

6. Erik Seidenfaden, *The Thai Peoples,* Siam Society, Bangkok, 1967, p. 118.

7. Over the last hundred years, several different missionary groups have produced written forms for many of the tribal languages, and Christian Bibles and other books are gradually being translated into and published in these languages. Some groups of Karen and Lisu in Burma have been literate for several generations as a result of missionary work there.

8. The Lahu story is retold from Elaine Lewis, "New Year — Lahu Style", *Sawaddi,* Nov.-Dec. 1974. p. 15.

9. Chob Kacha-ananda, "The Akha Swinging Ceremony", *JSS* 59 Part 1. Jan. 1970, p. 119.

10. Elaine Lewis, "New Year — Lahu Style", *Sawaddi,* Nov.-Dec. 1974, p. 15.

11. This story is told in Boon Chuey Srisavasdi, *The Hilltribes of Siam,* Nai Sura Saranakhom, Bangkok, 1967, p. 14.

12. Information on Karen tattooing can be found in E.M. Hinton, "The Dress of the Pwo Karen of Northern Thailand", *JSS* April 1974, p. 31.

13. Information on Karen tattooing comes from Peter Kunstadter, "Living with Thailand's Gentle Lua", *National Geographic Magazine* 130:1 (July 1966) p. 137.

14. This belief is recorded in Thamalot and Phuu Mii-Lot, *The Historical Background and Tradition of the Meo,* Chuan Printing Press, Bangkok, 1968. p. 10.

15. Further details on Lawa dress can be found in Sally Kunstadter's article, "Life among the Lawa", *Sawaddi,* February, 1965.

16. The most authoritative work on the dress of the Pwo Karen has been done by E.M. Hinton who describes her observations in "The dress of the Pwo Karen", *JSS* April 1974, pp. 27-50.

17. Quoted from the above article, p. 34.

18. For a detailed examination of Yao designs, their history and significance, see Jacqueline Butler, *Yao Design,* Siam Society, Bangkok, 1970.

19. E.M. Hinton, "The Dress of the Pwo Karen", *JSS* April, 1974, p. 32.

20. Gordon Young, *The Hilltribes of Northern Thailand,* Siam Society, Bangkok, 1974, p. 7.

21. Perhaps the most interesting use of rings can be seen in a photograph in Boon Chuey Srisavasdi's book, *The Hill Tribes of Siam.* On page 156, a Lawa girl is pictured wearing a belt made from dozens of the conical rings usually worn by the Akha, indicating, perhaps, the role of silver as a meeting point of tribal culture.

22. Gordon Young, *The Hilltribes of Northern Thailand,* p. 14.

BIBLIOGRAPHY

Many books, thesis and articles have been consulted in the course of the research for this book, but few of them have included any discussion of the crafts. Therefore, only those which make direct reference to the crafts are included in this bibliography, together with a very few key reference books. Detailed bibliographies on all other aspects of the hilltribes can be obtained from the National Library of Thailand, Samsen Road, Bangkok 3, or from the Tribal Research Centre, University of Chiang Mai, Chiang Mai, Thailand.

BOOKS

Butler, Jacqueline   *Yao Design*
Siam Society, Bangkok, 1970. 35 pages. A detailed examination of Yao embroidery and designs and their meanings.

Chindarsi, Nusit	The Religion of the Hmong Njua, Siam Society, Bankok, 1976.
Hearn, Robert M.	A six year collection of selected articles and clippings dealing with refugees and hilltribes in Northern Thailand during the period 1967-1972. USOM, Bangkok, 1972.
Lyman, Thomas Amis	Dictionary of Mong Njua. A Miao (Meo) Language of Southeast Asia. Mouton, The Hague and Paris, 1974.
Lebar, Frank M. **Gerald C. Hickey** **John K. Musgrave**	Ethnic Groups of Mainland Southeast Asia. Human Relations Area Files Press, New Haven, 1964.
McFarland, George Bradley, M.D.	Thai-English Dictionary, Stanford University Press, 1960.
Seidenfaden, Erik	*The Thai Peoples* Siam Society, Bangkok, 1967. 162 pages. First published in 1958, this includes a small section on hilltribe people and a few interesting old photos.
Srisavasdi, Boon Chuey	*The Hill Tribes of Siam* Nai Sura Saranakhom, Bangkok, 1967. 203 pages. A black and white photographic survey of the tribes with short explanatory paragraphs.
	Thirty Tribes in Chieng Rai. Nang Aroon Srisavasdi, Bangkok, 1955. (Thai language)
Thamalot and Phuu Mii-Lot	*The Historical Background and Tradition of the Meo,* Chuan Printing Press, Bangkok, 1968.
Tribal Research Centre	*Tribesmen and Peasants in North Thailand* Tribal Research Centre, Chiang Mai, 1969. Proceedings of the first symposium, 1967.
Wongprasert, Sanit	Preliminary Knowledge and Determination of Lahu Social Behaviour. Nai Boonlue Jaroenwong, Bangkok, 1976. (Thai language)
Young, Gordon	*The Hilltribes of Northern Thailand* Siam Society, Bangkok, 1974 (5th edition) 96 pages.

The most complete survey of the hilltribes presently available.

————————

Tracks of an Intruder
Souvenir Press, London, 1967. 191 pages. An account of a hunter's experiences in hilltribe country, including details on the weapons and hunting methods of tribes.

The Times Atlas of the World, Comprehensive Edition. The Times, in collaboration with John Bartholomew and Son. London, 1973.

————————

ARTICLES

Arritola, Marlene	"Hilltribe Silver Jewellry", *Sawaddi,* Nov.-Dec. 1972, pp. 15-18.
Calloway, Lois E.	"The Yao — Neighbours from Antiquity", *Sawaddi,* Feb. 1965, pp.
Durongkadej, Sripen	The Migration and Adult Education at Baan Mai Rom Yen. Unpublished paper. The Centre of Graduate Volunteers, Thammasat University, 1974. (Thai language)
Hinton, E.M.	"The Dress of the Pwo Karen of Northern Thailand", *Journal of the Siam Society* (JSS) April 1974, pp. 27-50.
Kacha-ananda, Chob	"The Akha Swinging Ceremony", *JSS* 59 Part 1, Jan. 1970, pp. 119-128.
Kauffman, H.E.	"Stone Memorials of the Lawa (Northwest Thailand)", *JSS* 59 Part 1, Jan. 1971, pp. 129-147.
Kunstadter, Peter	"Living with Thailand's Gentle Lua", *National Geographic Magazine,* 130:1, July 1966, pp. 122-152.
Kunstadter, Sally	"Life Among the Lawa", *Sawaddi,* Feb. 1965, pp. 7-8, 20-21.
Layton, Dora H.	"Heavenly Trousers", *Sawaddi,* April 1968, pp. 10-12, 26-27.
Lewis, Elaine	"The Linguistically Rich Akhas", *Sawaddi,* Jan.-Feb. 1969, pp. 8-10.
————————	"New Year — Lahu Style", *Sawaddi,* Nov.-Dec. 1974, pp. 14-16.

Lewis, Paul "An Akha for a Day", *Sawaddi*, Nov.-Dec. 1974 pp. 21-24.

Morse, Ron "The Lisu of Thailand", *Sawaddi*, Nov.-Dec. 1974 pp. 17-20.

Na Thalarng, Wasun The Society and Culture of the Akha at Doi Pa Mee, Mae Sai, Chieng Rai. Unpublished paper. The Centre of Graduate Volunteers, Thammasat University, 1974. (Thai language)

Seidenfaden, Erik "Siam's Tribal Dresses", *JSS* 31:Part 2, 1939, pp. 169-75.

Walker, Anthony R. "Blessing Feasts and Ancestor Propitiation among the Lahu Nyi (Red Lahu)", *JSS* 60:Part 1, Jan. 1972, pp. 345-73. "The Lahu Nyi (Red Lahu) New Year Celebrations" *JSS* 58: Part 1, Jan. 1970, pp. 1-44.

Thesis: "Lahu Nyi (Red Lahu): Village Society and Economy in Northern Thailand", Vols. I and II Report submitted to the Tribal Research Centre 1970.